GW01185015

# Digital Techniques 2 Checkbook

**J O Bird**
BSc(Hons), AFIMA, TEng(CEI), MITE

**A J C May**
BA, CEng, MIMechE, FITE, MBIM

**Butterworths**
London Boston Sydney Wellington Durban Toronto

First published 1982

© Butterworth & Co (Publishers) Ltd, 1982

---

**British Library Cataloguing in Publication Data**

Bird, J.O.
   Digital techniques 2 checkbook. — (Butterworths checkbook series)
   1. Digital electronics
   I. Title II. May, A.J.C.
   621.3815  TK868.D5

   ISBN 0-408-00674 9

---

Typeset by Scribe Design, Gillingham, Kent
Printed in England by Hartnoll Print Ltd., Bodmin, Cornwall

# Contents

# Note to Reader

As textbooks become more expensive, authors are often asked to reduce the number of worked and unworked problems, examples and case studies. This may reduce costs, but it can be at the expense of practical work which gives point to the theory.

Checkbooks if anything lean the other way. They let problem-solving establish and exemplify the theory contained in technician syllabuses. The Checkbook reader can gain *real* understanding through seeing problems solved and through solving problems himself.

Checkbooks do not supplant fuller textbooks, but rather supplement them with an alternative emphasis and an ample provision of worked and unworked problems. The brief outline of essential data—definitions, formulae, laws, regulations, codes of practice, standards, conventions, procedures, etc—will be a useful introduction to a course and a valuable aid to revision. Short-answer and multi-choice problems are a valuable feature of many Checkbooks, together with conventional problems and answers.

Checkbook authors are carefully selected. Most are experienced and successful technical writers; all are experts in their own subjects; but a more important qualification still is their ability to demonstrate and teach the solution of problems in their particular branch of technology, mathematics or science.

Authors, General Editors and Publishers are partners in this major low-priced series whose essence is captured by the Checkbook symbol of a question or problem 'checked' by a tick for correct solution.

# Preface

This textbook of worked problems provides coverage of the Technician Education Council level 2 half unit in Digital Techniques (syllabus U81/750). However it can be regarded as a basic textbook in Digital Techniques for a wider range of courses.

The aim of the book is to develop an understanding of binary arithmetic, Boolean algebra and logic elements.

Each topic considered in the text is presented in a way that assumes in the reader only the knowledge attained at TEC level 1 in Mathematics (U80/683, formerly U75/005).

This practical digital techniques book contains some 34 illustrations, nearly 50 detailed worked problems, followed by some 100 further problems with answers.

The authors would like to express their appreciation for the friendly co-operation and helpful advice given to them by the publishers. Thanks are due to Mrs Elaine Woolley for the excellent typing of the manuscript.

Finally, the authors would like to add a word of thanks to their wives, Elizabeth and Juliet, for their patience, help and encouragement during the preparation of this book.

JO Bird
AJC May
Highbury College of Technology
Portsmouth

# Butterworths Technical and Scientific Checkbooks

*General Editors for Science, Engineering and Mathematics titles:*
**J.O. Bird and A.J.C. May,** Highbury College of Technology, Portsmouth.

*General Editor for Building, Civil Engineering, Surveying and Architectural titles:*
**Colin R. Bassett,** lately of Guildford County College of Technology.

A comprehensive range of Checkbooks will be available to cover the major syllabus areas of the TEC, SCOTEC and similar examining authorities. A comprehensive list is given below and classified according to levels.

*Level 1 (Red covers)*
Mathematics
Physical Science
Physics
Construction Drawing
Construction Technology
Microelectronic Systems
Engineering Drawing
Workshop Processes & Materials

*Level 2 (Blue covers)*
Mathematics
Chemistry
Physics
Building Science and Materials
Construction Technology
Electrical & Electronic Applications
Electrical & Electronic Principles
Electronics
Microelectronic Systems
Engineering Drawing
Engineering Science
Manufacturing Technology
Digital Techniques
Motor Vehicle Science

*Level 3 (Yellow covers)*
Mathematics
Chemistry
Building Measurement
Construction Technology
Environmental Science
Electrical Principles
Electronics
Microelectronic Systems
Electrical Science
Mechanical Science
Engineering Mathematics & Science
Engineering Science
Engineering Design
Manufacturing Technology
Motor Vehicle Science
Light Current Applications

*Level 4 (Green covers)*
Mathematics
Building Law
Building Services & Equipment
Construction Technology
Construction Site Studies
Concrete Technology
Economics for the Construction Industry
Geotechnics
Engineering Instrumentation & Control

*Level 5*
Building Services & Equipment
Construction Technology
Manufacturing Technology

# 1 Conversion of denary numbers to binary numbers and vice versa

## A. MAIN POINTS CONCERNING THE CONVERSION OF DENARY NUMBERS TO BINARY NUMBERS AND VICE VERSA

1   (i)  The system of numbers in everyday use is the **denary** or **decimal** system of numbers, using the digits 0 to 9. It has ten different digits (0, 1, 2, 3, 4, 5, 6, 7, 8 and 9), and is said to have a **radix** or **base** of 10.

  (ii)  The binary system of numbers has a radix of 2 and uses only the digits 0 and 1.

2   (i)  The denary number 234.5 is equivalent to

$$2 \times 10^2 + 3 \times 10^1 + 4 \times 10^0 + 5 \times 10^{-1}$$

i.e., is the sum of terms comprising: (a digit) multiplied by (the base raised to some power).

  (ii)  In the binary system of numbers, the base is 2, so 1 101.1 is equivalent to:

$$1 \times 2^3 + 1 \times 2^2 + 0 \times 2^1 + 1 \times 2^0 + 1 \times 2^{-1}$$

Thus the denary number equivalent to the binary number 1 101.1 is

$8+4+0+1+\frac{1}{2}$ , that is 13.5,

i.e., $1\ 101.1_2 = 13.5_{10}$, the suffixes 2 and 10 denoting binary and denary systems of numbers respectively (see *Problems 1 to 3*).

3  An integer denary number can be converted to a corresponding binary number by repeatedly dividing by 2 and noting the remainder at each stage, as shown below for $39_{10}$.

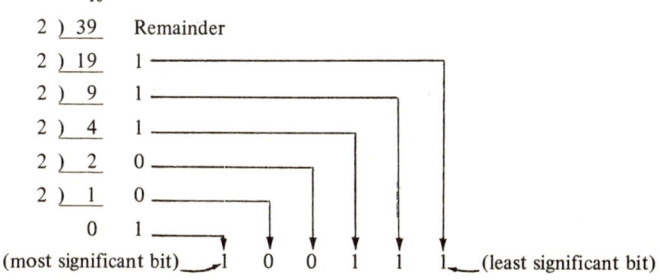

The result is obtained by writing the top digit of the remainder as the least significant bit, (a bit is a <u>b</u>inary dig<u>it</u> and the least significant bit is the one on the right). The bottom bit of the remainder is the most significant bit, i.e., the bit on the left.

Thus $39_{10} = 100\,111_2$

4  The fractional part of a denary number can be converted to a binary number by repeatedly multiplying by 2, as shown below for the fraction 0.625.

$$0.625 \times 2 = \quad 1.\,250$$
$$0.250 \times 2 = \quad 0.\,500$$
$$0.500 \times 2 = \quad 1.\,000$$

(most significant bit) 1 0 1 (least significant bit)

For fractions, the most significant bit of the result is the top bit obtained from the integer part of multiplication by 2. The least significant bit of the result is the bottom bit obtained from the integer part of multiplication by 2. Thus $0.625_{10} = 0.101_2$ (see *Problems 4 to 6*).

5  For denary integers containing several digits, repeatedly dividing by 2 can be a lengthy process. In this case, it is easier usually to convert a denary number to a binary number via the octal system of numbers. This system has a radix of 8, using the digits 0, 1, 2, 3, 4, 5, 6 and 7. The denary number equivalent to the octal number $4\,317_8$ is

$$4 \times 8^3 + 3 \times 8^2 + 1 \times 8^1 + 7 \times 8^0$$

i.e., $4 \times 512 + 3 \times 64 + 1 \times 8 + 7 \times 1$ or $2\,255_{10}$.

6  An integer denary number can be converted to a corresponding octal number by repeatedly dividing by 8 and noting the remainder at each stage, as shown below for $493_{10}$.

$$
\begin{array}{llll}
8 & ) & 493 & \text{Remainder} \\
8 & ) & 61 & 5 \\
8 & ) & 7 & 5 \\
& & 0 & 7 \\
\end{array}
$$

7 5 5

Thus $493_{10} = 755_8$

7  The fractional part of a denary number can be converted to an octal number by repeatedly multiplying by 8, as shown below for the fraction $0.4375_{10}$.

$$0.4375 \times 8 = \quad 3\,.\,5$$
$$0.5 \times 8 = \quad 4\,.\,0$$

.3 4

For fractions, the most significant bit is the top integer obtained by multiplication of the denary fraction by 8, thus

$$0.4375_{10} = 0.34_8$$

8  The natural binary code for digits 0 to 7 is shown in *Table 1*, and an octal number

2

**TABLE 1**

| Octal digit | Natural binary number |
|:-----------:|:---------------------:|
| 0 | 000 |
| 1 | 001 |
| 2 | 010 |
| 3 | 011 |
| 4 | 100 |
| 5 | 101 |
| 6 | 110 |
| 7 | 111 |

can be converted to a binary number by writing down the three bits corresponding to the octal digit.

Thus $437_8 = 100\,011\,111_2$
and $26.35_8 = 010\,110\,.\,011\,101_2$

The '0' on the extreme left does not signify anything, thus

$26.35_8 = 10\,110\,.\,011\,101_2$

To convert a denary number to a binary number via octal, the denary number is first converted to an octal number, as shown in paras 6 and 7, and then the corresponding binary number is written down, as shown in para 8 (see *Problems 7 to 9*).

## B. WORKED PROBLEMS ON THE CONVERSION OF DENARY NUMBERS TO BINARY NUMBERS AND VICE VERSA

*Problem 1* Convert $11\,011_2$ to a denary number.

From para 2:
$$11\,011_2 = 1 \times 2^4 + 1 \times 2^3 + 0 \times 2^2 + 1 \times 2^1 + 1 \times 2^0$$
$$= 16 + 8 + 0 + 2 + 1$$
$$= 27_{10}$$

*Problem 2* Convert $0.1011_2$ to a denary fraction.

From para 2:

$$0.1011_2 = 1 \times 2^{-1} + 0 \times 2^{-2} + 1 \times 2^{-3} + 1 \times 2^{-4}$$

$$= 1 \times \frac{1}{2} + 0 \times \frac{1}{2^2} + 1 \times \frac{1}{2^3} + 1 \times \frac{1}{2^4}$$

$$= \frac{1}{2} + \frac{1}{8} + \frac{1}{16}$$

$$= 0.5 + 0.125 + 0.0625$$

$$= 0.6875_{10}$$

*Problem 3* Convert $101.0101_2$ to a denary number.

From para 2:
$$101.0101_2 = 1 \times 2^2 + 0 \times 2^1 + 1 \times 2^0 + 0 \times 2^{-1} + 1 \times 2^{-2} + 0 \times 2^{-3} + 1 \times 2^{-4}$$
$$= 4 + 0 + 1 + 0 + 0.25 + 0 + 0.0625$$
$$= 5.3125_{10}$$

*Problem 4* Convert $47_{10}$ to a binary number.

From para 3, repeatedly dividing by 2 and noting the remainder gives:

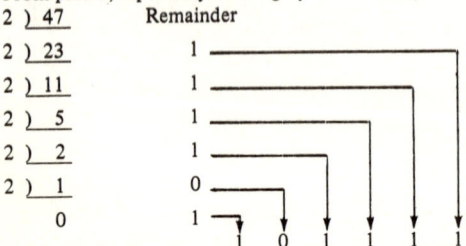

Thus $47_{10} = 101\ 111_2$

*Problem 5* Convert $0.40625_{10}$ to a binary number

From para 4, repeatedly multiplying by 2 gives:

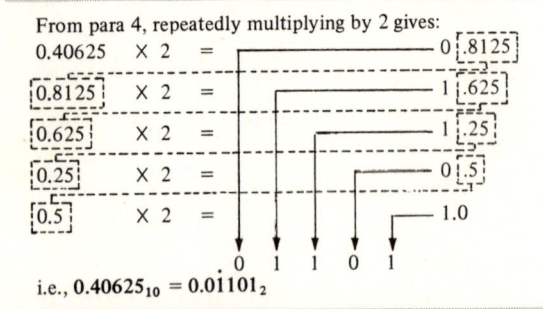

i.e., $0.40625_{10} = 0.01101_2$

*Problem 6* Convert $58.3125_{10}$ to a binary number.

The integer part is repeatedly divided by 2, giving:

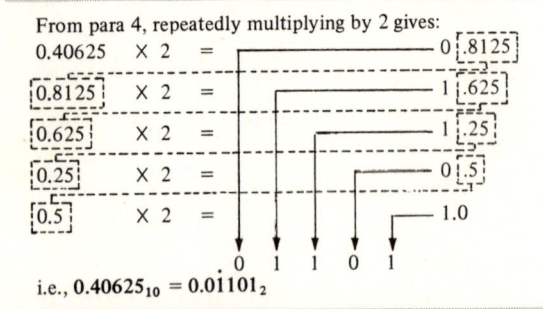

The fractional part is repeatedly multiplied by 2 giving:

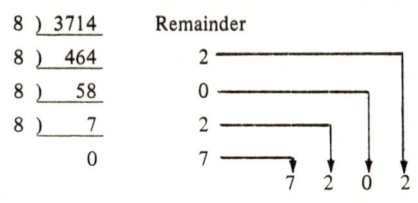

$$0.3125 \times 2 = 0.625$$
$$0.625 \times 2 = 1.25$$
$$0.25 \times 2 = 0.5$$
$$0.5 \times 2 = 1.0$$
$$. \quad 0 \quad 1 \quad 0 \quad 1$$

Thus $58.3125_{10} = 111\ 010.0101_2$

*Problem* 7 Convert $3714_{10}$ to a binary number, via octal.

Dividing repeatedly by 8, noting the remainder gives:

| 8 ) 3714 | Remainder |
|---|---|
| 8 ) 464 | 2 |
| 8 ) 58 | 0 |
| 8 ) 7 | 2 |
| 0 | 7 |

$$7 \quad 2 \quad 0 \quad 2$$

From *Table 1*, $7202_8 = 111\ 010\ 000\ 010_2$
i.e., $3714_{10} = 111\ 010\ 000\ 010_2$

*Problem* 8 Convert $0.59375_{10}$ to a binary number, via octal.

Multiplying repeatedly by 8, noting the integer values, gives:

$$0.59375 \times 8 = 4.75$$
$$0.75 \times 8 = 6.00$$
$$. \quad 4 \quad 6$$

Thus $0.59375_{10} = 0.46_8$
From *Table 1*, $0.46_8 = 0.100\ 110_2$
i.e. $0.59375_{10} = 0.100\ 11_2$

*Problem* 9 Convert $5613.90625_{10}$ to a binary number, via octal.

The integer part is repeatedly divided by 8, noting the remainder, giving:

| 8 ) 5613 | Remainder |
|---|---|
| 8 ) 701 | 5 |
| 8 ) 87 | 5 |
| 8 ) 10 | 7 |
| 8 ) 1 | 2 |
| 0 | 1 |

$$1 \quad 2 \quad 7 \quad 5 \quad 5$$

This octal number is converted to a binary number, (see *Table 1*).

$$12755_8 = 001\ 010\ 111\ 101\ 101_2$$

i.e. $\quad 5613_{10} = 1\ 010\ 111\ 101\ 101_2$

The fractional part is repeatedly multiplied by 8, noting the integer part, giving:

$0.90625 \times 8 = \qquad 7.25$

$0.25 \quad \times 8 = \qquad 2.00$

This octal fraction is converted to a binary number, (see *Table 1*)

$0.72_8 = 0.111\ 010_2$

i.e. $\quad 0.90625_{10} = 0.111\ 01_2$

**Thus, $5613.90625_{10} = 1\ 010\ 111\ 101\ 101.111\ 01_2$**

*Problem 10* Convert $11\ 110\ 011.100\ 01_2$ to a denary number via octal.

Grouping the binary number in three's from the binary point gives:

$011\ 110\ 011.100\ 010_2$

Using *Table 1* to convert this binary number to an octal number gives:
$363.42_8$
From para 5:
$$363.42_8 = 3 \times 8^2 + 6 \times 8^1 + 3 \times 8^0 + 4 \times 8^{-1} + 2 \times 8^{-2}$$
$$= 192 + 48 + 3 + 0.5 + 0.03125$$
$$= 243.53125_{10}$$

## C. FURTHER PROBLEMS ON THE CONVERSION OF DENARY NUMBERS TO BINARY NUMBERS AND VICE VERSA

In *Problems 1 to 4*, convert the binary numbers given to denary numbers.

1 (a) 110, (b) 1011, (c) 1110, (d) 1001 $\qquad$ [(a) $6_{10}$, (b) $11_{10}$, (c) $14_{10}$, (d) $9_{10}$]

2 (a) 10 101, (b) 11 001, (c) 101 101, (d) 110 011

$\qquad$ [(a) $21_{10}$, (b) $25_{10}$, (c) $45_{10}$, (d) $51_{10}$]

3 (a) 0.1101, (b) 0.11001, (c) 0.00111, (d) 0.01011

$\qquad$ [(a) $0.8125_{10}$, (b) $0.78125_{10}$, (c) $0.21875_{10}$, (d) $0.34375_{10}$]

4 (a) 11010.11, (b) 10111.011, (c) 110101.0111, (d) 11010101.10111

$\qquad$ [(a) $26.75_{10}$, (b) $23.375_{10}$, (c) $53.4375_{10}$, (d) $213.71875_{10}$]

In *Problems 5 to 8*, convert the denary numbers given to binary numbers.

5 (a) 5, (b) 15, (c) 17, (d) 29 $\quad$ [(a) $101_2$, (b) $1\ 111_2$, (c) $10\ 001_2$, (d) $11\ 101_2$]

6 (a) 31, (b) 42, (c) 57, (d) 63

$\qquad$ [(a) $11\ 111_2$, (b) $101\ 010_2$, (c) $111\ 001_2$, (d) $111\ 111_2$]

7 (a) 0.25, (b) 0.21875, (c) 0.28125, (d) 0.59375

$\qquad$ [(a) $0.01_2$, (b) $0.001\ 11_2$, (c) $0.010\ 01_2$, (d) $0.100\ 11_2$]

8 (a) 47.40625, (b) 30.8125, (c) 53.90625, (d) 61.65625

$\qquad$ [(a) $101\ 111.011\ 01_2$, (b) $11\ 110.110\ 1_2$, (c) $110\ 101.111\ 01_2$,

(d) $111\ 101.101\ 01_2$]

In *Problems 9 to 11*, convert the denary numbers given to binary numbers, via octal.

9 (a) 343, (b) 572, (c) 1 265

$$[(a)\ 101\ 010\ 111_2,\ (b)\ 1\ 000\ 111\ 100_2,\ (c)\ 10\ 011\ 110\ 001_2]$$

10 (a) 0.46875, (b) 0.6875, (c) 0.71875

$$[(a)\ 0.011\ 11_2,\ (b)\ 0.101\ 1_2,\ (c)\ 0.101\ 11_2]$$

11 (a) 247.09375, (b) 514.4375, (c) 1716.78125

$$[(a)\ 11\ 110\ 111.000\ 11_2,\ (b)\ 1\ 000\ 000\ 010.011\ 1_2,\ (c)\ 11\ 010\ 110\ 100.110\ 01_2]$$

12 Convert the binary numbers given to denary numbers via octal.

(a) 111.011 1, (b) 101 001.01, (c) 1 110 011 011 010.001 1

$$[(a)\ 7.4375_{10},\ (b)\ 41.25_{10},\ (c)\ 7386.1875_{10}]$$

# 2 Addition and subtraction of binary numbers

## A. MAIN POINTS CONCERNING THE ADDITION AND SUBTRACTION OF BINARY NUMBERS

1  Binary addition of two bits is achieved according to the following rules:

|  |  |  |  | Sum | Carry |
|---|---|---|---|---|---|
| 0 | + | 0 | = | 0 | 0 |
| 0 | + | 1 | = | 1 | 0 |
| 1 | + | 0 | = | 1 | 0 |
| 1 | + | 1 | = | 0 | 1 |

When adding binary numbers A and B, A is called the **augend** and B is called the **addend**. For example, adding 1 and 1 produces a sum of 0 and a carry of 1, and may be laid out as shown below.

| Augend | 1 |
|---|---|
| Addend | 1 |
| Sum | 0 |
| Carry | 1 |

2  Binary addition of three bits, (augend + addend + carry) is achieved according to the following rules:

|  |  |  |  |  |  | Sum | Carry |
|---|---|---|---|---|---|---|---|
| 0 | + | 0 | + | 0 | = | 0 | 0 |
| 0 | + | 0 | + | 1 | = | 1 | 0 |
| 0 | + | 1 | + | 0 | = | 1 | 0 |
| 0 | + | 1 | + | 1 | = | 0 | 1 |
| 1 | + | 0 | + | 0 | = | 1 | 0 |
| 1 | + | 0 | + | 1 | = | 0 | 1 |
| 1 | + | 1 | + | 0 | = | 0 | 1 |
| 1 | + | 1 | + | 1 | = | 1 | 1 |

Using the rules of two bit and three bit addition, two binary numbers say 1011 and 1110, may be added as shown:

| Column | 5 | 4 | 3 | 2 | 1 |
|---|---|---|---|---|---|
| Augend |  | 0 | 1 | 0 | 1 | 1 |
| Addend |  | 0 | 1 | 1 | 1 | 0 |
| Sum |  | 1 | 1 | 0 | 0 | 1 |
| Carry | 0 | 1 | 1 | 1 | 0 |

Column 1: Adding augend and addend gives $1 + 0 =$ sum 1, carry 0 to column 2.
Column 2: Adding augend, addend and carry gives: $1 + 1 + 0 =$ sum 0, carry 1 to column 3.
Column 3: Adding augend, addend and carry gives: $0 + 1 + 1 =$ sum 0, carry 1 to column 4, and so on.

(See *Problems 1 to 3*)

3 A negative binary number can be stored in a calculator or computer by using a sign bit to denote the negative quantity. Binary numbers having a sign bit are called **signed-magnitude** binary numbers. An additional bit is allocated to the left of the binary number to indicate the sign and by convention, a sign bit of 0 is used to denote a positive number and a 1 to denote a negative number. Thus, in a signed-bit system, (0) $1001_2$ represents the denary number $+9$, but (1) $1001_2$ represents the denary number $-9$, the sign bit being shown in brackets. Signed-magnitude binary numbers have two parts: (i) the sign bit (shown in brackets in this chapter for clarity), giving the sign of the number, and (ii) a binary number following the sign bit giving the size or **modulus** of the binary number. One of the disadvantages of a signed-bit system is that it reduces the maximum number capable of being stored in a given sized register by approximately a half. For example, a 4-bit register can store the positive numbers 0 to 15 if no sign bit is used, and the numbers $-7$ to $+7$ when a sign bit is used.

4 In many calculators, microprocessors and computers, the process of subtracting one binary number from another is performed by a process called complementary addition. This process enables the same logic circuitry to be used for both addition and subtraction. There are two methods of complementary addition in widespread use: (i) the **one's complement** method, shown in para 5, and (ii) the **two's complement** method, shown in para 6.

5 **The one's complement method.**
When subtracting binary number B from binary number A, i.e. $A-B = C$, A is called the **minuend**, B is called the **subtrahend** and C is called the **difference**, i.e., **minuend** $-$ **subtrahend** $=$ **difference**. The procedure for subtracting one binary number from another using the one's complement method is as follows:
   (i) Express both minuend and subtrahend so that they each have the same number of bits.
  (ii) Determine the one's complement of the subtrahend. This is achieved by writing 1 for 0 and 0 for 1 for each bit in the subtrahend. Thus the one's complement of 101 101 is 010 010.
 (iii) Add the minuend to the one's complement of the subtrahend to obtain a sum.
 (iv) Depending on the number of bits in the sum, the result of complementary addition, using the one's complement method is obtained thus:
     (a) If the sum has the same number of bits as the minuend and subtrahend of (i), the difference between the minuend and subtrahend is negative, and the value is the one's complement of the sum.
     (b) If one extra bit is generated in the sum by complementary addition in (iii), the difference between the minuend and subtrahend is positive and its value is given by **end-around carry**, that is, by taking the bit on the extreme left of the sum and adding it to the bit on the extreme right. Thus, end-around carry operating on 1 001 011 gives 1 100 as shown:

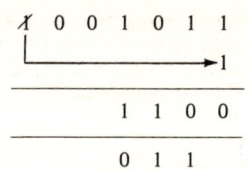

$$0 \quad 1 \quad 1$$

*Problems 4 to 7* illustrate the process of subtraction by the one's complement method.

6 **The two's complement method**

Assuming the subtraction is of the form:

minuend − subtrahend = difference,

then the procedure for determining the difference by the two's complement method is as follows:

(i) Express the minuend and subtrahend so that they each have the same number of bits.

(ii) Add the sign-bit, (0) for a positive number and (1) for a negative number on the extreme left of both the minuend and subtrahend.

[Note: 10 111 − 101 means that both minuend and subtrahend are positive numbers, i.e., (+10 111) − (+101) and are assigned sign-bits of (0).]

(iii) Determine the two's complement of the subtrahend. This is achieved by writing down the one's complement and adding 1. Thus the two's complement of 101 011 is 010 100 + 1, i.e., 010 101.

(iv) Add the minuend to the two's complement of the subtrahend to obtain a sum.

(v) Depending on whether the sign bit is (0) or (1), the result of complementary addition by the two's complement method is obtained thus:

(a) If the sign bit is (0), the 1 on the left of the sign is disregarded and the difference between the minuend and subtrahend is positive and its value is given by the bits to the right of the sign bit in the sum.

(b) If the sign bit is (1), the difference between the minuend and subtrahend is negative and its value is the two's complement of the sum.

*Problems 8 to 11* illustrate the process of subtraction by the two's complement method.

7 **Binary subtraction** of two numbers may also be achieved by a method of direct subtraction, according to the rules:

|  |  | difference | borrow |
|---|---|---|---|
| 0 − 0 | = | 0 | 0 |
| 0 − 1 | = | 1 | 1 |
| 1 − 0 | = | 1 | 0 |
| 1 − 1 | = | 0 | 0 |

Thus, the method of taking $1011_2$ from $1101_2$ is as shown, the subtraction for each column being: minuend − (subtrahend + borrow).

| Column | 5 | 4 | 3 | 2 | 1 |
|---|---|---|---|---|---|
| Minuend |  | 1 | 1 | 0 | 1 |
| Subtrahend |  | 1 | 0 | 1 | 1 |
| Difference |  | 0 | 0 | 1 | 0 |
| Borrow | 0 | 0 | 1 | 0 | 0 |

Column 1: $1 - (1 + 0) = $ difference 0, borrow 0 (in column 2).
Column 2: $0 - (1 + 0) = $ difference 1, borrow 1 (in column 3).
Column 3: $1 - (0 + 1) = $ difference 0, borrow 0 (in column 4).
Column 4: $1 - (1 + 0) = $ difference 0, borrow 0 (in column 5).

Thus $1101_2 - 1011_2 = 10_2$.

In practice, the procedure is much the same as subtraction in denary numbers. To take $1011_2$ from $1101_2$ is as shown:

| Column | 4 | 3 | 2 | 1 |
|---|---|---|---|---|
| Minuend | 1 | $^0\!1$ | $^2\!\emptyset$ | 1 |
| Subtrahend | 1 | 0 | 1 | 1 |
| Difference | 0 | 0 | 1 | 0 |

Column 1: $1 - 1 = $ difference 0.
Column 2: $0 - 1$, borrow 1 from column 3 leaving the minuend of column 3 as 0. The borrowed 1 becomes 2 when moved to column 2. $2 - 1 = $ difference 1.
Column 3: $0 - 0 = $ difference 0.
Column 4: $1 - 1 = $ difference 0.
Thus, $1101_2 - 1011_2 = 10_2$, as obtained previously.

## B. WORKED PROBLEMS ON THE ADDITION AND SUBTRACTION OF BINARY NUMBERS

*Problem 1* Add $11011_2$ and $10110_2$.

The rules for binary addition are given in paras 1 and 2.

| Column | 6 | 5 | 4 | 3 | 2 | 1 |
|---|---|---|---|---|---|---|
| Augend | 0 | 1 | 1 | 0 | 1 | 1 |
| Addend | 0 | 1 | 0 | 1 | 1 | 0 |
| Sum | 1 | 1 | 0 | 0 | 0 | 1 |
| Carry | 0 | 1 | 1 | 1 | 1 | 0 |

Column 1: Using the rules for two-bit addition, $1 + 0 = $ sum 1, carry 0.
The rules for three-bit addition are used for the remaining columns, applied to augend + addend + carry.
Column 2: $1 + 1 + 0 = $ sum 0, carry 1.
Column 3: $0 + 1 + 1 = $ sum 0, carry 1.
Column 4: $1 + 0 + 1 = $ sum 0, carry 1.
Column 5: $1 + 1 + 1 = $ sum 1, carry 1.
Column 6: $0 + 0 + 1 = $ sum 1, carry 0.

Thus $11\,011_2 + 10\,110_2 = 110\,001_2$

*Problem 2* Add the compound binary numbers $1\,101.101\,1_2$ and $101.010\,1_2$.

The rules for binary addition given in paras 1 and 2 apply to fractional parts of binary numbers as well as integer binary numbers.

| Column | 9 | 8 | 7 | 6 | 5 | | 4 | 3 | 2 | 1 |
|---|---|---|---|---|---|---|---|---|---|---|
| Augend | 0 | 1 | 1 | 0 | 1 | . | 1 | 0 | 1 | 1 |
| Addend | 0 | 0 | 1 | 0 | 1 | . | 0 | 1 | 0 | 1 |
| Sum | 1 | 0 | 0 | 1 | 1 | . | 0 | 0 | 0 | 0 |
| Carry | 1 | 1 | 0 | 1 | 1 | . | 1 | 1 | 1 | |

Column 1: Using the rules for two-bit addition gives $1 + 1 =$ sum 0, carry 1, (to column 2).

Adding augend, addend and carry for the remaining columns gives:

Column 2: $1 + 0 + 1 =$ sum 0, carry 1, (to column 3),
Column 3: $0 + 1 + 1 =$ sum 0, carry 1, (to column 4).
Column 4: $1 + 0 + 1 =$ sum 0, carry 1, (to column 5).
Column 5: $1 + 1 + 1 =$ sum 1, carry 1, (to column 6).
Column 6: $0 + 0 + 1 =$ sum 1, carry 0.
Column 7: $1 + 1 + 0 =$ sum 0, carry 1.
Column 8: $1 + 0 + 1 =$ sum 0, carry 1.
Column 9: $0 + 0 + 1 =$ sum 1.

**Thus $1\,101.101\,1_2 + 101.010\,1_2 = 10\,011.000\,0_2 = 10\,011_2$**

*Problem 3* Use binary addition to find the value of $10\,110_2 + 11\,101_2 + 11\,101_2$.

This addition may be achieved by adding $10\,110_2$ to $11\,101_2$ as shown in *Problems 1 and 2*, and then adding $11\,101_2$ to this result. Alternatively, direct addition may be achieved as shown.

| Column | 7 | 6 | 5 | 4 | 3 | 2 | 1 |
|---|---|---|---|---|---|---|---|
| | 0 | 0 | 1 | 0 | 1 | 1 | 0 |
| | 0 | 0 | 1 | 1 | 1 | 0 | 1 |
| | 0 | 0 | 1 | 1 | 1 | 0 | 1 |
| Sum | 1 | 0 | 1 | 0 | 0 | 0 | 0 |
| Carry | | 1 | 2 | 2 | 2 | 1 | 1 |

Column 1: $0 + 1 + 1 =$ sum 0, carry 1 to column 2.
Column 2: $1 + 0 + 0 + 1$ (carry) $=$ sum 0, carry 1 to column 3.
Column 3: $1 + 1 + 1 + 1$ (carry) $= 4$. Just as $1 + 1 = 2$, which is sum 0, carry 1.
$1 + 1 + 1 + 1 = 4$, which is sum 0, carry 2,
$1 + 1 + 1 + 1 + 1 = 5$, which is sum 1, carry 2, and so on.

Thus $1 + 1 + 1 + 1$ (carry) $=$ sum 0, carry 2 to column 4.
Column 4: $0 + 1 + 1 + 2$ (carry) $=$ sum 0, carry 2 to column 5.
Column 5: $1 + 1 + 1 + 2$ (carry) $=$ sum 1, carry 2 to column 6.
Column 6: $0 + 0 + 0 + 2$ (carry) $=$ sum 0, carry 1 to column 7.
Column 7: $0 + 0 + 0 + 1$ (carry) $=$ sum 1, carry 0.

**Thus $10\,110_2 + 11\,101_2 + 11\,101_2 = 1\,010\,000_2$**

*Problem 4* Determine the value of $1\ 011_2 - 110_2$ by the one's complement method.

The procedure given in para 5 is followed for a minuend of 1 011 and a subtrahend of 110.

(i)  $1\ 011 - 110 = 1\ 011 - 0\ 110$.
(ii) The one's complement of the subtrahend is 1 001.
(iii) Adding the minuend and the one's complement of the subtrahend gives:

$$
\begin{array}{r}
1\ 011 \\
\underline{1\ 001} \\
\end{array}
$$

Sum    10 100

(iv) An extra bit is generated in the sum so the procedure given in para 5 (iv)(b) is adopted. The difference is positive and its value is obtained by 'end-around carry', i.e.,

1̸0 100

└──→1

Sum        101

**Thus $1\ 011_2 - 110_2 = 101_2$**

*Problem 5* Use the one's complement method to find the value of $10\ 011_2 - 11\ 010_2$.

The procedure given in para 5 is followed for a minuend of 10 011 and a subtrahend of 11 010.
(i)  This step is not necessary since both minuend and subtrahend have the same number of bits.
(ii) The one's complement of the subtrahend is 00 101.
(iii) Adding the minuend and one's complement of the subtrahend gives:

$$
\begin{array}{r}
10\ 011 \\
\underline{00\ 101} \\
\end{array}
$$

Sum        11 000

(iv) The sum has the same number of bits as the minuend and subtrahend, hence para 5(iv)(a) applies. The difference is negative and its value is the one's complement of the sum, i.e. $-00\ 111$

**Thus $10\ 011_2 - 11\ 010_2 = -111_2$**

*Problem 6* Use the one's complement method to find the value of $11\ 101_2 - 1\ 110_2$.

Using the procedure given in para 5 gives:
(i)  $11\ 101 - 1\ 110 = 11\ 101 - 01\ 110$

(ii) The one's complement of the subtrahend is 10 001.

(iii) Adding the minuend and one's complement of the subtrahend gives:

$$11\ 101$$
$$10\ 001$$

Sum    $101\ 110$

(iv) Using end-around-carry, since an extra list has been generated, gives:

$$\cancel{1}01\ 110$$

$$\longrightarrow 1$$

$$1\ 111$$

**Thus $11\ 101_2 - 1\ 110_2 = 1\ 111_2$**

*Problem 7* Determine the value of $100\ 101_2 - 101\ 101_2$ by using the one's complement method.

The procedure given in para 5 is used.

(i) Not applicable.

(ii) The one's complement of the subtrahend is 010 010.

(iii) Adding the minuend and one's complement of the subtrahend gives:

$$100\ 101$$
$$010\ 010$$

Sum    $110\ 111$

(iv) No extra bit has been generated, hence the required difference is negative and is the one's complement of the sum, i.e. $-001\ 000$

**Thus $100\ 101_2 - 101\ 101_2 = -1\ 000_2$**

*Problem 8* Use the two's complement method to find the value of $1\ 101\ 011_2 - 110\ 100_2$.

The procedure given in para 6 is followed for a minuend of 1 101 011 and a subtrahend of 110 100.

(i) $1\ 101\ 011 - 110\ 100 = 1\ 101\ 011 - 0\ 110\ 100$.

(ii) Adding the sign bits gives (0) 1 101 011 $-$ (0) 0 110 100, the sign bit being (0) since both numbers are positive, i.e. $(+1\ 101\ 011_2) - (+110\ 100_2)$.

(iii) The two's complement of the subtrahend is obtained from the one's complement plus one, i.e. (1) 1 001 011 + 1, that is, (1) 1 001 100.

(iv) Adding the minuend and two's complement of the subtrahend gives:

$$(0)\ 1\ 101\ 011$$
$$(1)\ 1\ 001\ 100$$

Sum    $1(0)\ 0\ 110\ 111$

(v) The sign bit is (0), hence para 6(v)(a) applies. The 1 on the left of the sign bit is disregarded, the difference is positive and its value is given by the bits on the right of the sign bit,

$$1\ 101\ 011_2 - 110\ 100_2 = 110\ 111_2$$

*Problem 9* Determine the value of $101\ 101_2 - 110\ 110_2$ by using the two's complement method.

The procedure given in para 6 is followed.
(i) This step is not necessary since both minuend and subtrahend have the same number of bits.
(ii) Adding the sign bits gives $(0)\ 101\ 101 - (0)\ 110\ 110$.
(iii) The two's complement of the subtrahend is $(1)\ 001\ 001 + 1$, i.e. $(1)\ 001\ 010$.
(iv) Adding the minuend and the two's complement of the subtrahend gives:

$$
\begin{array}{ll}
& (0)\ 101\ 101 \\
& (1)\ 001\ 010 \\
\hline
\text{Sum} & (1)\ 110\ 111 \\
\hline
\end{array}
$$

(v) The sign bit is (1), hence para 6(v)(b) applies. The difference is negative and the value is the two's complement of the sum, i.e.,

$$101\ 101_2 - 110\ 110_2 = -(0)\ 001\ 000 + 1 = -1\ 001_2$$

*Problem 10* Find the value of $1\ 100\ 101_2 - 111\ 010_2$ by using the two's complement method. Check the answer obtained by using a method of direct subtraction.

The procedure given in para 6 is used.
(i) $1\ 100\ 101 - 111\ 010 = 1\ 100\ 101 - 0\ 111\ 010$
(ii) The sign bits are added, giving

$$(0)\ 1\ 100\ 101 - (0)\ 0\ 111\ 010$$

(iii) The two's complement of the subtrahend is

$$(1)\ 1\ 000\ 101 + 1, \text{ i.e. } (1)\ 1\ 000\ 110.$$

(iv) Adding the minuend and two's complement of the subtrahend gives:

$$
\begin{array}{ll}
& (0)\ 1\ 100\ 101 \\
& (1)\ 1\ 000\ 110 \\
\hline
\text{Sum} & 1(0)\ 0\ 101\ 011 \\
\hline
\end{array}
$$

(v) Since the sign bit is (0), the answer is positive and the 1 on the left of the sign bit is disregarded. Hence

$$1\ 100\ 101_2 - 111\ 010_2 = 101\ 011_2$$

Checking by direct subtraction:

| column | 7 | 6 | 5 | 4 | 3 | 2 | 1 |
|---|---|---|---|---|---|---|---|
| minuend | $\not{1}$ | $\not{1}^{\,0\,2}$ | 0 | $\not{1}^{\,1\,2}$ | $0$ | $\not{1}^{\,0\,2}$ | 1 |
| subtrahend | | 1 | 1 | 1 | 0 | 1 | 0 |
| | | 1 | 0 | 1 | 0 | 1 | 1 |

| Column 1: | $1 - 0 = 1.$ |
| Column 2: | $0 - 1.$  Borrow 1 from column 3. A 1 moving from a column to an adjacent column on its right becomes a 2. Hence $2 - 1 = 1.$ |
| Column 3: | $0 - 0 = 0.$ |
| Column 4: | $0 - 1.$  Borrow 1 from column 6. This becomes 2 in column 5 and one of these is then borrowed for column 4. Hence $2 - 1 = 1.$ |
| Column 5: | $1 - 1 = 0.$ |
| Column 6: | $0 - 1.$  Borrow 1 from column 7. $2 - 1 = 1.$ |

Thus $1\,100\,101_2 - 111\,010_2 = 101\,011_2$, as obtained previously.

*Problem 11* Use the two's complement method to find the value of $1\,010\,111_2 - 1\,110\,010_2$.

The procedure given in para 6 is used.

(i) Not applicable.

(ii) Adding the sign bits gives $(0)\,1\,010\,111 - (0)\,1\,110\,010$

(iii) The two's complement of the subtrahend is

$(1)\,0\,001\,101 + 1$, i.e. $(1)\,0\,001\,110.$

(iv) Adding the minuend and the two's complement of the subtrahend gives

$(0)\,1\,010\,111$

$(1)\,0\,001\,110$

Sum$\qquad(1)\,1\,100\,101$

(v) The sign bit is (1), hence the required difference is negative and its modulus is the two's complement of the sum.

Thus $1\,010\,111_2 - 1\,110\,010_2 = -(0)\,0\,011\,010 + 1$
$= -11\,011_2$

## C.  FURTHER PROBLEMS ON THE ADDITION AND SUBTRACTION OF BINARY NUMBERS

In *Problems 1 to 8*, evaluate in binary form.

| 1 | $110\,110_2 + 101\,010_2$ | $[1\,100\,000_2]$ |
| 2 | $1\,011\,101_2 + 1\,101\,101_2$ | $[11\,001\,010_2]$ |
| 3 | $11\,101\,111_2 + 10\,100\,011_2$ | $[110\,010\,010_2]$ |
| 4 | $100.001\,1_2 + 1.100\,11_2$ | $[101.110\,01_2]$ |
| 5 | $10\,110\,001.101_2 + 10\,110\,110.011\,1_2$ | $[101\,101\,000.0001_2]$ |
| 6 | $11\,010_2 + 1\,011_2 + 10\,111_2$ | $[111\,100_2]$ |
| 7 | $111\,010_2 + 10\,101_2 + 11\,101_2 + 10\,110_2$ | $[10\,000\,010_2]$ |
| 8 | $1\,010_2 + 1\,011_2 + 1\,100_2 + 1\,111_2 + 10\,111_2$ | $[1\,000\,111_2]$ |

In *Problems 9 to 13*, use the one's complement method to find the values required. Check the result obtained by a method of direct subtraction.

| 9 | $1\,101_2 - 110_2$ | $[111_2]$ |
| 10 | $1\,101\,001_2 - 1\,011\,100_2$ | $[1\,101_2]$ |

11 $101\ 100\ 011_2 - 1\ 101\ 101_2$ $\hspace{4cm}$ $[11\ 110\ 110_2]$
12 $110\ 010\ 010_2 - 11\ 101\ 111_2$ $\hspace{4cm}$ $[10\ 100\ 011_2]$
13 $101\ 011\ 101_2 - 110\ 110\ 011_2$ $\hspace{4cm}$ $[-1\ 010\ 110_2]$

In *Problems 14 to 18*, use the two's complement method to find the values required.
Check the result obtained by a method of direct subtraction.

14 $11\ 010_2 - 1\ 011_2$ $\hspace{4cm}$ $[1\ 111_2]$
15 $110\ 101_2 - 101\ 010_2$ $\hspace{4cm}$ $[1\ 011_2]$
16 $1\ 010\ 001_2 - 1\ 100\ 101_2$ $\hspace{4cm}$ $[-10\ 100_2]$
17 $10\ 110\ 101_2 - 1\ 001\ 101_2$ $\hspace{4cm}$ $[1\ 101\ 000_2]$
18 $10\ 111\ 010_2 - 11\ 010\ 110_2$ $\hspace{4cm}$ $[-11\ 100_2]$

# 3 Multiplication and division of binary numbers

## A. MAIN POINTS CONCERNING THE MULTIPLICATION AND DIVISION OF BINARY NUMBERS

1 Binary multiplication of two bits is according to the following rules:

$$0 \times 0 = 0$$
$$0 \times 1 = 0$$
$$1 \times 0 = 0$$
$$1 \times 1 = 1$$

When multiplying A by B to give C, i.e. $A \times B = C$, A is called the **multiplicand**, B the **multiplier** and C the **product**.

2 The operation of multiplication in binary is similar to that for denary numbers, as shown below for $14_{10} \times 6_{10}$.

| $14_{10} =$ | | | | 1 | 1 | 1 | $0_2$ | (multiplicand) |
|---|---|---|---|---|---|---|---|---|
| $6_{10} =$ | | | | 0 | 1 | 1 | $0_2$ | (multiplier) |
| | | | | 0 | 0 | 0 | 0 | |
| | | | 1 | 1 | 1 | 0 | | |
| | | 1 | 1 | 1 | 0 | | | |
| | 0 | 0 | 0 | 0 | | | | |
| $84_{10} =$ | 1 | 0 | 1 | 0 | 1 | 0 | $0_2$ | (product) |

It can be seen that zero bits in the multiplier do not contribute to the product and are usually ignored. Thus, binary multiplication of $25_{10} \times 13_{10}$ is performed as shown.

| $25_{10} =$ | | | 1 | 1 | 0 | 0 | 1 | (multiplicand) |
|---|---|---|---|---|---|---|---|---|
| $13_{10} =$ | | | 1 | 1 | 0 | 1 | | (multiplier) |
| | | | 1 | 1 | 0 | 0 | 1 | |
| | 1 | 1 | 0 | 0 | 1 | | | |
| | 1 | 1 | 0 | 0 | 1 | | | |
| $325_{10} =$ | 1 | 0 | 1 | 0 | 0 | 0 | 1 | 0 | 1 | (product) |

3 Denary multiplication of numbers having decimal fractions is performed by ignoring the decimal point in the first instance and then counting the number of fractional digits in both the multiplicand and multiplier to position the decimal point in the product. Thus:

$$31.4_{10} \times 13.72_{10} = 430.808_{10}$$

A similar procedure is used for binary numbers. Thus $12\frac{1}{2}_{10} \times 9\frac{3}{8}_{10}$ in binary multiplication gives:

| | | | |
|---|---|---|---|
| $12\frac{1}{2}_{10}$ = | 1 1 0 0 . 1 | | (multiplicand) |
| $9\frac{3}{8}_{10}$ = | 1 0 0 1 . 0 1 1 | | (multiplier) |
| | 1 1    0 0 1 | | |
| | 1 1 0    0 1 | | (partial |
| | 1 1 0 0 1 | | products) |
| | 1 1 0 0 1 | | |
| $117.187\,5_{10}$ = | 1 1 1 0 1 0 1 . 0 0 1 1 | | (product) |

(Should it occur when adding the partial products,
$1 + 1 + 1 + 1 = 0$, carry 2; $1 + 1 + 1 + 1 + 1 = 1$, carry 2; and so on.)

4 The process of multiplication can be performed by adding the multiplicand to itself as many times as required by the multiplier, thus

$$9_{10} \times 4_{10} = 9_{10} + 9_{10} + 9_{10} + 9_{10} = 36_{10}$$

Similarly, in binary numbers

$$1011_2 \times 101_2 = 1011_2 + 1011_2 + 1011_2 + 1011_2 + 1011_2 \text{ (since } 101_2 = 5_{10})$$

Using the principles introduced in Chapter 2:

| | | | | | | |
|---|---|---|---|---|---|---|
| | 0 | 0 | 1 | 0 | 1 | 1 |
| | 0 | 0 | 1 | 0 | 1 | 1 |
| | 0 | 0 | 1 | 0 | 1 | 1 |
| | 0 | 0 | 1 | 0 | 1 | 1 |
| | 0 | 0 | 1 | 0 | 1 | 1 |
| Sum | 1 | 1 | 0 | 1 | 1 | 1 |
| Carry | 1 | 3 | 1 | 3 | 2 | |

i.e. $\mathbf{1011_2 \times 101_2 = 110\,111_2}$

For binary mixed numbers, the position of the binary point is ignored in the first instance, multiplication by repeated addition is performed as shown above and the binary point is inserted after multiplication, (see para 3).
Thus:

$101.1_2 \times 1.01_2$ is treated as $1011_2 \times 101_2$ in the first instance,
i.e. $1011_2 \times 101_2 = 110\,111_2$, (see above) and $101.1_2 \times 1.01_2 = 110.111_2$,
(from para 3).
(See *Problems 1 to 3*.)

5 When dividing number A by number B, giving C and remainder D, i.e.,

$\dfrac{A}{B} = C$, remainder D, A is called the **dividend**, B the **divisor** and C the **quotient**.

To perform $51_{10} \div 9_{10}$ in binary, a similar procedure to that for long division of denary numbers is used.

$$51_{10} = 110\,011_2$$
$$9_{10} = \phantom{00}1\,001_2$$

```
                                1  0  1        (quotient)
(divisor)   1  0  0  1  )  1  1  0  0  1  1     (dividend)
                           1  0  0  1
                        ─────────────────
                           0  0  1  1  1  1
                                 1  0  0  1
                           ─────────────────
                                 1  1  0
```

Thus $\dfrac{110\,011_2}{1\,001_2} = 101_2$, remainder $110_2$.

(Complementary addition may be used as an alternative to direct binary subtraction, see Chapter 2.)

6 Binary mixed numbers can be dealt with by expressing them as whole binary numbers. Thus

$$\dfrac{10\,110.01_2}{1010.1_2} = \dfrac{10\,110\,01_2}{1010\,10_2} \quad , \text{ and dividing as shown in para 5, gives:}$$

```
                              1  0
    1  0  1  0  1  0  )  1  0  1  1  0  0  0  1
                        1  0  1  0  1  0
                        ────────────────────
                        0  0  0  0  1  0  1
```

i.e. $\dfrac{1\,011\,001}{101\,010} = 10_2 + \dfrac{101_2}{101\,010_2}$

$$= 10_2 + \dfrac{1.01_2}{1010.1_2}$$

$$= 10_2 \text{, remainder } 1.01_2$$

7 Binary division may be performed by repeated addition of the divisor. For example:

$$\dfrac{12_{10}}{3_{10}} = \dfrac{1100_2}{11_2}$$

Repeated addition of the divisor gives:

$$
\begin{array}{ll}
11 & \text{once} \\
\underline{11} & \text{twice} \\
110 & \\
\underline{11} & \text{three times} \\
1001 & \\
\underline{11} & \text{four times} \quad = \quad 4 = 100_2. \\
1100, & \text{i.e., the dividend}
\end{array}
$$

Thus, $\dfrac{1100_2}{11_2} = 100_2$

Similarly, $\dfrac{1110_2}{11_2}$ gives

$$
\begin{array}{ll}
11 & \text{once} \\
\underline{11} & \text{twice} \\
110 & \\
\underline{11} & \text{three times} \\
1001 & \\
\underline{11} & \text{four times} \\
1100 & \\
\underline{11} & \text{five times} \\
1111 & \text{which is larger than the dividend.}
\end{array}
$$

The number 1100, (the four times product) is larger than $1110_2$ by $10_2$.

Thus, $\dfrac{1110_2}{11_2} = 100_2$, remainder $10_2$

(See *Problems 4 to 7.*)

## B. WORKED PROBLEMS ON THE MULTIPLICATION AND DIVISION OF BINARY NUMBERS

*Problem 1* Determine the value of $1\,011\,010_2 \times 101\,101_2$

Using the principles introduced in para 2, gives:

```
(multiplicand)          1 0 1 1 0 1 0
(multiplier)              1 0 1 1 0 1
                        _____
                          1 0 1 1 0 1 0
                        1 0 1 1 0 1 0
                      1 0 1 1 0 1 0
                    1 0 1 1 0 1 0
                    _____
(Product)           1 1 1 1 1 1 0 1 0 0 1 0
```

Note: in the seventh column from the right, $1 + 1 + 1 + 1 + 1$ (carry) is sum 1, carry 2.

Thus $1\,011\,010_2 \times 101\,101_2 = 111\,111\,010\,010_2$

(Check: $90_{10} \times 45_{10} = 4\,050_{10}$)

**Problem 2** Find the value of $101\,011.101_2 \times 10\,111.11_2$

With reference to para 3, the binary points are ignored in the first instance, but a binary point must be inserted five places from the right in the solution. Thus:

```
(multiplicand)          101 011 101
(multiplier              1 011 111
                        _____
                        101 011 101
                       1 010 111 01
                      10 101 110 1
                       101 011 101
                      1 010 111 01
                      101 011 101
                    _____
Product             1 000 000 110 000 011
                    _____
Carry               1 122 333 343 321 00
```

so, $101\,011\,101_2 \times 1\,011\,111_2 = 1\,000\,000\,110\,000\,011_2$

and $101\,011.101_2 \times 10\,111.11_2 = 10\,000\,001\,100.000\,11_2$

**Problem 3** Use a process of repeated addition to show that $10\,111_2 \times 101_2 = 1\,110\,011_2$

Adding $10\,111_2$ to itself $101_2$ times, that is five times, gives:

```
                          010 111
                          010 111
                          010 111
                          010 111
                          010 111
                        _____
Sum                     1 110 011
                        _____
Carry                   1 324 32
```

When adding the column on the extreme right, $1 + 1 + 1 + 1 + 1$ gives 5, that is, sum 1, carry 2. The next column is $1 + 1 + 1 + 1 + 1 + 2$ (carry), that is 7, i.e. sum 1, carry 3, and so on.

Thus $10\,111_2 + 10\,111_2 + \ldots\ldots$ to 5 terms $= 1\,110\,011_2$

**Problem 4** Divide $121_{10}$ by $11_{10}$ in binary.

$$121_{10} = 1\,111\,001_2$$

and $\quad 11_{10} = \quad\ \ 1\,011_2$

Using the principles introduced in para 5, this gives:

```
                              1  0 1 1     (quotient)
(divisor)           1   0 1 1 ) 1  1 1 1  0 0 1     (dividend)
                              1  0 1 1
                               0 1 1 1 1 1
                              1 0 0 0 0 0 2
                                1 0  1 1
                                1 0  1 1
                                1 0  1 1
                                0 0  0 0
```

Thus $\dfrac{1\,111\,001_2}{1\,011_2} = 1\,011_2$, remainder 0

**Problem 5** Divide $101\,101.1_2$ by $1\,101.11_2$

Expressing the mixed binary numbers as integers gives: $\dfrac{10\,110\,110_2}{110\,111_2}$

Using the principles introduced in para 5, gives:

```
                              1 1
1 1 0   1 1 1 ) 1 0  1 1 0  1 1 0
                1  1 0 1  1 1
                1 0 0 1 0  1 1 0 2
                  1 1 0  1 1 1
                  1 0  0 0 1
```

Thus $\dfrac{10\,110\,110_2}{110\,111_2} = 11_2 + \dfrac{10\,001}{110\,111} = 11_2 + \dfrac{100.01}{1\,101.11}$

$$= 11_2,\ \text{remainder } 100.01_2$$

**Problem 6** Divide $101\,010_2$ by $111_2$ by a process of repeated addition

Adding the divisor to itself repeatedly gives:

23

| (divisor) | | |
|---|---|---|
| | 111 | once |
| | 111 | twice |
| | 1 110 | |
| | 111 | three times |
| | 10 101 | |
| | 111 | four times |
| | 11 100 | |
| | 111 | five times |
| | 100 011 | |
| | 111 | six times |
| (dividend) | 101 010 | |

Six times in binary is $110_2$, hence

$$\frac{101\ 010_2}{111_2} = 110_2, \text{ by repeated addition of the divisor}$$

*Problem 7* Divide $100\ 110_2$ by $1\ 001_2$ by a process of repeated addition.

Using the same method as in *Problem 6* above gives:

| | | |
|---|---|---|
| | 1 001 | once |
| | 1 001 | twice |
| | 10 010 | |
| | 1 001 | three times |
| | 11 011 | |
| | 1 001 | four times |
| | 100 100 | |
| | 1 001 | five times |
| | 101 101 | |

The result of adding $1\ 001_2$ to itself five times is $101\ 101_2$ which is larger than the dividend $100\ 110_2$. Hence $\dfrac{100\ 110_2}{1\ 001_2}$ goes four times, and the remainder is $100\ 110_2 - 100\ 100_2$, i.e. $10_2$.

Thus $\dfrac{100\ 110_2}{1\ 001_2} = 100_2$, remainder $10_2$

## C. FURTHER PROBLEMS ON THE MULTIPLICATION AND DIVISION OF BINARY NUMBERS

In *Problems 1 to 10*, determine the products by using binary multiplication, expressing the result in both binary and denary forms.

1  $1\ 001_2 \times 1\ 000_2$  $\hfill [1\ 001\ 000_2\ ;\ 72]$
2  $11\ 011_2 \times 111_2$  $\hfill [10\ 111\ 101_2\ ;\ 189]$
3  $11\ 001_2 \times 1\ 101_2$  $\hfill [101\ 000\ 101_2\ ;\ 325]$
4  $110\ 100_2 \times 1\ 011_2$  $\hfill [1\ 000\ 111\ 100_2\ ;\ 572]$
5  $10\ 011_2 \times 101\ 100_2$  $\hfill [1\ 101\ 000\ 100_2\ ;\ 836]$

6  $110.1_2 \times 1\ 010.111_2$  $\hfill [1\ 000\ 110.101\ 1_2\ ;\ 70\frac{11}{16}]$

7  $10\ 100_2 \times 100.011_2$  $\hfill [1\ 010\ 111.1_2\ ;\ 87\frac{1}{2}]$

8  $10\ 001.11_2 \times 1\ 101_2$  $\hfill [11\ 100\ 110.11_2\ ;\ 230\frac{3}{4}]$

9  $10\ 110.1_2 \times 10\ 111.011_2$  $\hfill [1\ 000\ 001\ 101.111\ 1_2\ ;\ 525\frac{15}{16}]$

10  $1\ 010.101_2 \times 110\ 001.1_2$  $\hfill [1\ 000\ 001\ 101.111\ 1_2\ ;\ 525\frac{15}{16}]$

In *Problems 11 to 20*, determine the quotients (and remainders) by binary division, expressing the answers in both binary and denary forms.

11  $10\ 100_2 \div 100_2$  $\hfill [101_2\ ;\ 5]$
12  $101\ 010_2 \div 111_2$  $\hfill [110_2\ ;\ 6]$
13  $1\ 001\ 101_2 \div 1\ 011_2$  $\hfill [111_2\ ;\ 7]$
14  $1\ 100\ 110_2 \div 110_2$  $\hfill [10\ 001_2\ ;\ 17]$
15  $110\ 110\ 101_2 \div 10\ 111_2$  $\hfill [10\ 011_2\ ;\ 19]$

16  $\dfrac{10\ 111_2}{100_2}$  $\hfill [101_2,\ \text{rem.}\ 11_2\ ;\ 5,\ \text{rem.}\ 3]$

17  $\dfrac{101\ 101_2}{1\ 000_2}$  $\hfill [101_2,\ \text{rem.}\ 101_2\ ;\ 5,\ \text{rem.}\ 5]$

18  $\dfrac{10\ 010\ 010_2}{10\ 000_2}$  $\hfill [1\ 001_2,\ \text{rem.}\ 10_2\ ;\ 9,\ \text{rem.}\ 2]$

19  $\dfrac{11\ 010.001_2}{100.11_2}$  $\hfill [101_2,\ \text{rem.}\ 10.011_2\ ;\ 5,\ \text{rem.}\ 2\frac{3}{8}]$

20  $\dfrac{1\ 101\ 000.101_2}{101.11_2}$  $\hfill [1\ 111_2,\ \text{rem.}\ 11.011_2\ ;\ 15,\ \text{rem.}\ 3\frac{3}{8}]$

# 4 Boolean algebra and switching circuits

## A. MAIN POINTS CONCERNED WITH BOOLEAN ALGEBRA AND SWITCHING CIRCUITS

1 A **two-state device** is one whose basic elements can have only one of two conditions. Thus, two-way switches, which can be either on or off, and the binary numbering system, having the digits 0 and 1 only, are two-state devices. In Boolean algebra, if $A$ represents one state, then $\overline{A}$, called 'not-$A$', represents the second state.

2 The **or**-function.
In Boolean algebra, the **or**-function for two elements $A$ and $B$ is written as $A + B$, and is defined as '$A$, or $B$, or both $A$ and $B$'. The equivalent electrical circuit for a two-input **or**-function is given by two switches connected in parallel. With reference to *Fig 1(a)* the lamp will be on when $A$ is on, or when $B$ is on, or when both $A$ and $B$ are on. In the table shown in *Fig 1(b)*, all the possible switch combinations are shown in columns 1 and 2, in which a 0 represents a switch being off and a 1 represents the switch being on, these columns being called the inputs. Column 3 is called the output and a 0 represents the lamp being off and a 1 represents the lamp being on. Such a table is called a **truth table**.

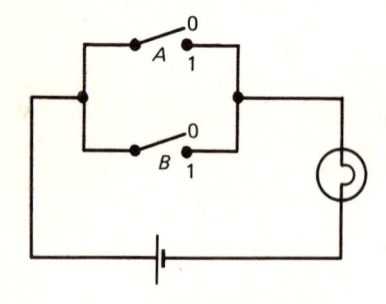

| 1 | 2 | 3 |
|---|---|---|
| Input (switches) | | Output (lamp) |
| $A$ | $B$ | $Z = A + B$ |
| 0 | 0 | 0 |
| 0 | 1 | 1 |
| 1 | 0 | 1 |
| 1 | 1 | 1 |

(a) Switching circuit for **or** — function

(b) Truth table for **or** — function

**Fig 1**

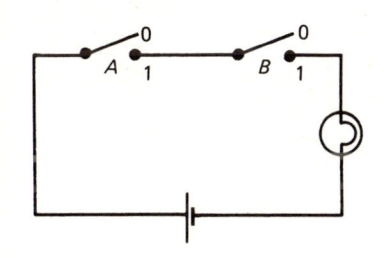

| Input (switches) | | Output (lamp) |
|---|---|---|
| $A$ | $B$ | $Z = A . B$ |
| 0 | 0 | 0 |
| 0 | 1 | 0 |
| 1 | 0 | 0 |
| 1 | 1 | 1 |

(a) Switching circuit for **and** − function  (b) Truth table for **and** − function

**Fig 2**

3 The **and**-function.
In Boolean algebra, the **and**-function for two elements $A$ and $B$ is written as $A.B$ and is defined as 'both $A$ and $B$'. The equivalent electrical circuit for a two-input **and**-function is given by two switches connected in series. With reference to *Fig 2(a)* the lamp will be on only when both $A$ and $B$ are on. The truth table for a two-input **and**-function is shown in *Fig 2(b)*.

4 The **not**-function.
In Boolean algebra, the **not**-function for element $A$ is written as $\overline{A}$, and is defined as 'the opposite to $A$'. Thus if $A$ means switch $A$ is on, $\overline{A}$ means that switch $A$ is off. The truth table for the **not**-function is shown in *Table 1*.

TABLE 1

| *Input* *A* | *Output* $Z = \overline{A}$ |
|---|---|
| 0 | 1 |
| 1 | 0 |

5 In paras 2, 3 and 4 above, the Boolean expressions, equivalent switching circuits and truth tables for three of the functions used in Boolean algebra are given for a two-input system. A system may have more than two inputs and the Boolean expression for a three-input **or**-function having elements $A$, $B$ and $C$ is $A+B+C$. Similarly, a three-input **and**-function is written as $A.B.C$. The equivalent electrical circuits and truth tables for three-input **or** and **and**-functions are shown in *Figs 3(a)* and *(b)* respectively.

6 To achieve a given output, it is often necessary to use combinations of switches connected both in series and in parallel. If the output from a switching circuit is given by the Boolean equation $Z = A.B + \overline{A}.\overline{B}$, the truth table is as shown in *Fig 4(a)*. In this table, columns 1 and 2 give all the possible combinations of $A$ and $B$. Column 3 corresponds to $A.B$ and column 4 to $\overline{A}.\overline{B}$, i.e. a 1 output is obtained when $A = 0$ and when $B = 0$. Column 5 is the **or**-function applied to columns 3 and 4 giving an output of $Z = A.B + \overline{A}.\overline{B}$. The corresponding switching circuit is shown in *Fig 4(b)* in which $A$ and $B$ are connected in series to give $A.B$; $\overline{A}$ and

27

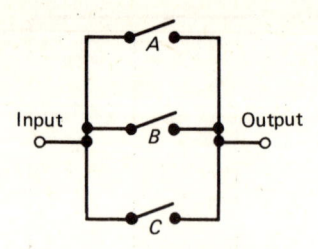

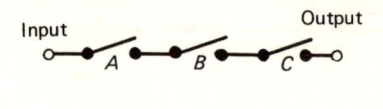

| Input | | | Output |
|---|---|---|---|
| $A$ | $B$ | $C$ | $Z = A + B + C$ |
| 0 | 0 | 0 | 0 |
| 0 | 0 | 1 | 1 |
| 0 | 1 | 0 | 1 |
| 0 | 1 | 1 | 1 |
| 1 | 0 | 0 | 1 |
| 1 | 0 | 1 | 1 |
| 1 | 1 | 0 | 1 |
| 1 | 1 | 1 | 1 |

| Input | | | Output |
|---|---|---|---|
| $A$ | $B$ | $C$ | $Z = A.B.C$ |
| 0 | 0 | 0 | 0 |
| 0 | 0 | 1 | 0 |
| 0 | 1 | 0 | 0 |
| 0 | 1 | 1 | 0 |
| 1 | 0 | 0 | 0 |
| 1 | 0 | 1 | 0 |
| 1 | 1 | 0 | 0 |
| 1 | 1 | 1 | 1 |

(a) The **or** — function electrical circuit and truth table

**Fig 3**

(b) The **and** — function electrical circuit and truth table

| 1 | 2 | 3 | 4 | 5 |
|---|---|---|---|---|
| $A$ | $B$ | $A.B$ | $\overline{A}.\overline{B}$ | $Z = AB + \overline{A}.\overline{B}$ |
| 0 | 0 | 0 | 1 | 1 |
| 0 | 1 | 0 | 0 | 0 |
| 1 | 0 | 0 | 0 | 0 |
| 1 | 1 | 1 | 0 | 1 |

(a) Truth table for $Z = A.B + \overline{A}.\overline{B}$

**Fig 4**

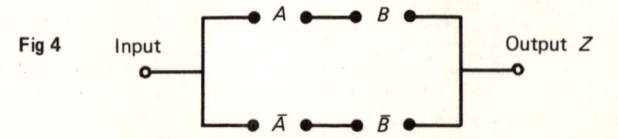

(b) Switching circuit for $Z = A.B + \overline{A}.\overline{B}$.

$\bar{B}$ are connected in series to give $\bar{A}.\bar{B}$, and $A.B$ and $\bar{A}.\bar{B}$ are connected in parallel to give $A.B+\bar{A}.\bar{B}$. The circuit symbols used are such that $A$ means the switch is on when $A$ is 1, $\bar{A}$ means the switch is on when $A$ is 0, and so on.

7 Often when describing a complex switching circuit by means of a Boolean equation, many terms and many elements per term are used. Frequently, the laws and rules of Boolean algebra may be used to simplify the Boolean expression and some of the laws and rules are given in *Table 2*, the derivation and verification of these laws being given in paras 8 to 12.

TABLE 2 Some Laws and Rules of Boolean Algebra

| Reference | Name | Rule or law |
|---|---|---|
| 1 2 | Commutative laws | $A+B = B+A$ $A.B = B.A$ |
| 3 4 | Associative laws | $(A+B)+C = A+(B+C)$ $(A.B).C = A.(B.C)$ |
| 5 6 | Distributive laws | $A.(B+C) = A.B+A.C$ $A+(B.C) = (A+B).(A+C)$ |
| 7 8 9 10 | Sum rules | $A+0 = A$ $A+1 = 1$ $A+A = A$ $A+\bar{A} = 1$ |
| 11 12 13 14 | Product rules | $A.0 = 0$ $A.1 = A$ $A.A = A$ $A.\bar{A} = 0$ |
| 15 | Double 'not' rule | $\bar{\bar{A}} = A$ |

TABLE 3

| 1 | 2 | 3 | 4 | 5 | 6 | 7 |
|---|---|---|---|---|---|---|
| A | B | C | $(A+B)$ | $(A+B)+C$ | $(B+C)$ | $A+(B+C)$ |
| 0 | 0 | 0 | 0 | 0 | 0 | 0 |
| 0 | 0 | 1 | 0 | 1 | 1 | 1 |
| 0 | 1 | 0 | 1 | 1 | 1 | 1 |
| 0 | 1 | 1 | 1 | 1 | 1 | 1 |
| 1 | 0 | 0 | 1 | 1 | 0 | 1 |
| 1 | 0 | 1 | 1 | 1 | 1 | 1 |
| 1 | 1 | 0 | 1 | 1 | 1 | 1 |
| 1 | 1 | 1 | 1 | 1 | 1 | 1 |

8 The **associative law** given in *Table 2*, $(A+B)+C = A+(B+C)$, can be verified as follows. With reference to *Table 3*:
Columns 1, 2 and 3 give all the possible inputs of $A$, $B$ and $C$.
Column 4 is obtained from the **or**-function applied to column 1 and 2.
Column 5 is the **or**-function applied to columns 3 and 4.
Column 6 is the **or**-function applied to columns 2 and 3.
Column 7 is the **or**-function applied to columns 1 and 6.

Since the pattern of 0s and 1s in columns 5 and 7 are the same, this verifies that $(A+B)+C = A+(B+C)$.

9 The **distributive law**, $A.(B+C) = A.B+A.C$, given in *Table 2* can be verified by using a truth table, shown in *Table 4*.

Columns 1 to 3 give all the possible inputs for $A$, $B$ and $C$.
Column 4 is the **or**-function applied to columns 2 and 3.
Column 5 is the **and**-function applied to columns 1 and 4.
Column 6 is the **and**-function applied to columns 1 and 2.
Column 7 is the **and**-function applied to columns 1 and 3.
Column 8 is the **or**-function applied to columns 6 and 7.
Since the outputs in columns 5 and 8 are the same, this verifies that $A.(B+C) = A.B+A.C$.

TABLE 4

| 1 | 2 | 3 | 4 | 5 | 6 | 7 | 8 |
|---|---|---|---|---|---|---|---|
| $A$ | $B$ | $C$ | $(B+C)$ | $A.(B+C)$ | $A.B$ | $A.C$ | $A.B+A.C$ |
| 0 | 0 | 0 | 0 | 0 | 0 | 0 | 0 |
| 0 | 0 | 1 | 1 | 0 | 0 | 0 | 0 |
| 0 | 1 | 0 | 1 | 0 | 0 | 0 | 0 |
| 0 | 1 | 1 | 1 | 0 | 0 | 0 | 0 |
| 1 | 0 | 0 | 0 | 0 | 0 | 0 | 0 |
| 1 | 0 | 1 | 1 | 1 | 0 | 1 | 1 |
| 1 | 1 | 0 | 1 | 1 | 1 | 0 | 1 |
| 1 | 1 | 1 | 1 | 1 | 1 | 1 | 1 |

10 The sum rules given in *Table 2* can be derived or verified by considering a parallel switching arrangement, where '0' means a switch is open and '1' means the switch is closed. The circuit for $A+0$ is shown in *Fig 5(a)*, and the corresponding truth table in *Fig 5(b)*. Since the output $Z$ has the same pattern of 0's and 1's as $A$, then $A+0 = A$. The other sum rules can be verified in a similar manner.

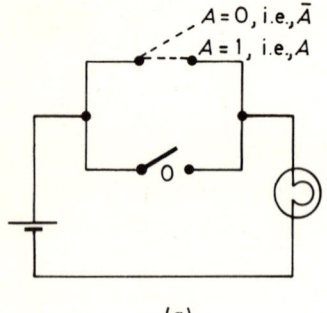

| $A$ | $0$ | $Z = A+0$ |
|---|---|---|
| 0 | 0 | 0 |
| 1 | 0 | 1 |

(b)

(a)          **Fig 5**

11 The product rules given in *Table 2* can be derived or verified by considering a series switching arrangement. The circuit for $A.1$ is shown in *Fig 6(a)* and the corresponding truth table in *Fig 6(b)*. Since the output $Z$ has the same pattern of 0's and 1's as $A$, then $A.1 = A$. The other product rules can be verified in a similar manner.

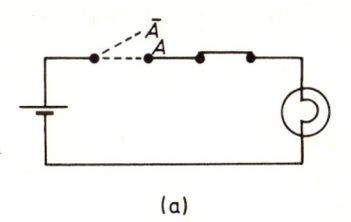

| $A$ | 1 | $Z = A.1$ |
|---|---|---|
| 0 | 1 | 0 |
| 1 | 1 | 1 |

(a)         (b)

**Fig 6**

TABLE 5

| 1 | 2 | 3 |
|---|---|---|
| $A$ | $\bar{A}$ | $\bar{\bar{A}}$ |
| 0 | 1 | 0 |
| 1 | 0 | 1 |

12 Rule 15 of *Table 2* can be verified by using a truth table, as shown in *Table 5*. Column 1 gives all the possibilities for $A$. Column 2 is the **not**-function applied to column 1. Column 3 is the **not**-function applied to column 2. Since columns 1 and 3 have the same pattern of 0's and 1's, then $\bar{\bar{A}} = A$.

## B. WORKED PROBLEMS ON BOOLEAN ALGEBRA AND SWITCHING CIRCUITS

*Problem 1* Derive the Boolean expression and construct a truth table for the switching circuit shown in *Fig 7(a)*.

The switches between 1 and 2 in *Fig 7(a)* are in series and have a Boolean expression of $B.A$. The parallel circuit, 1 to 2 and 3 to 4, have a Boolean expression of

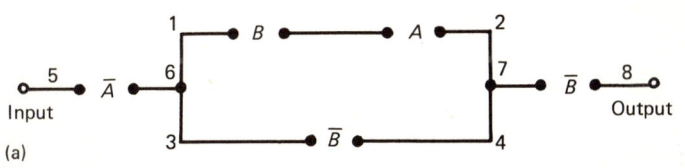

(a)

**Fig 7**

| 1 | 2 | 3 | 4 | 5 | 6 | 7 |
|---|---|---|---|---|---|---|
| $A$ | $B$ | $B.A$ | $\bar{B}$ | $B.A + \bar{B}$ | $\bar{A}$ | $Z = \bar{A}.(B.A + \bar{B}).\bar{B}$ |
| 0 | 0 | 0 | 1 | 1 | 1 | 1 |
| 0 | 1 | 0 | 0 | 0 | 1 | 0 |
| 1 | 0 | 0 | 1 | 1 | 0 | 0 |
| 1 | 1 | 1 | 0 | 1 | 0 | 0 |

(b)

$(B.A+\overline{B})$. The parallel circuit can be treated as a single switching unit, giving the equivalent of switches 5 to 6, 6 to 7 and 7 to 8 in series. Thus the output is given by

$$Z = \overline{A}.(B.A+\overline{B}).\overline{B}$$

The truth table is as shown in *Fig 7(b)*. Columns 1 and 2 give all the possible combinations of switches $A$ and $B$. Column 3 is the **and**-function applied to columns 1 and 2, giving $B.A$. Column 4 is $\overline{B}$, or the opposite to column 2. Column 5 is the **or**-function applied to columns 3 and 4. Column 6 is $\overline{A}$, or the opposite to column 1. The output is column 7 and is obtained by applying the **and**-function to columns 4, 5 and 6. From the truth table, a 1 output is obtained when $A = 0$ and $B = 0$, (i.e. when $\overline{A} = 1$ and $\overline{B} = 1$), that is along path 5, 6, 3, 4, 7, 8.

*Problem 2* Derive the Boolean equation and construct a truth table for the switching circuit shown in *Fig 8(a)*.

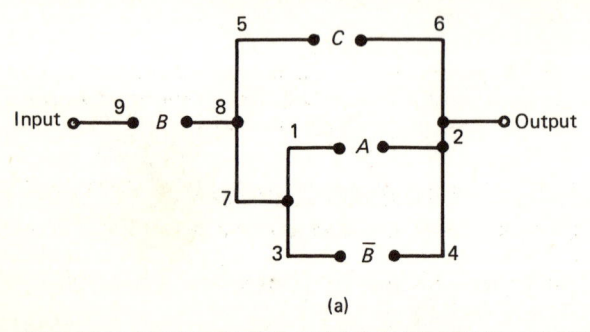

(a)

| 1 | 2 | 3 | 4 | 5 | 6 | 7 |
|---|---|---|---|---|---|---|
| $A$ | $B$ | $C$ | $\overline{B}$ | $A+\overline{B}$ | $C+(A+\overline{B})$ | $Z=B.[C+(A+\overline{B})]$ |
| 0 | 0 | 0 | 1 | 1 | 1 | 0 |
| 0 | 0 | 1 | 1 | 1 | 1 | 0 |
| 0 | 1 | 0 | 0 | 0 | 0 | 0 |
| 0 | 1 | 1 | 0 | 0 | 1 | 1 |
| 1 | 0 | 0 | 1 | 1 | 1 | 0 |
| 1 | 0 | 1 | 1 | 1 | 1 | 0 |
| 1 | 1 | 0 | 0 | 1 | 1 | 1 |
| 1 | 1 | 1 | 0 | 1 | 1 | 1 |

**Fig 8**                  (b)

The parallel circuit, 1 to 2 and 3 to 4, gives $(A+\overline{B})$ and this is equivalent to a single switching unit between 7 and 2. The parallel circuit 5 to 6 and 7 to 2 gives $C+(A+\overline{B})$ and this is equivalent to a single switching unit between 8 and 2. The series circuit 9 to 8 and 8 to 2 gives the output $Z = B.[C+(A+\overline{B})]$.

The truth table is shown in *Fig 8(b)*. Columns 1, 2 and 3 give all the possible combination of $A$, $B$ and $C$. Column 4 is $\overline{B}$ and is the opposite to column 2. Column 5 is the **or**-function applied to columns 1 and 4, giving $(A+\overline{B})$. Column 6 is the **or**-function applied to columns 3 and 5 giving $C+(A+\overline{B})$. The output is given in column 7 and is obtained by applying the **and**-function to columns 2 and 6, giving $Z = B.[C+(A+\overline{B})]$.

> *Problem 3* Construct a switching circuit to meet the requirements of the Boolean equation: $Z = A.\overline{C}+\overline{A}.B+\overline{A}.B.\overline{C}$. Construct the truth table for this circuit.

The three terms joined by **or**-functions (+), indicate three parallel branches having:

| | branch 1 | $A$ **and** $\overline{C}$ in series |
|---|---|---|
| | branch 2 | $\overline{A}$ **and** $B$ in series |
| and | branch 3 | $\overline{A}$ **and** $B$ **and** $\overline{C}$ in series. |

Hence the required switching circuit is as shown in *Fig 9(a)*.

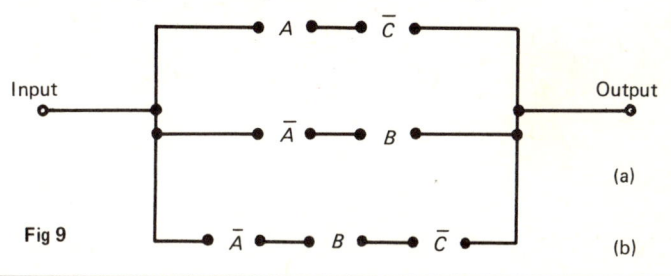

Fig 9

(a)

(b)

| 1<br>$A$ | 2<br>$B$ | 3<br>$C$ | 4<br>$\overline{C}$ | 5<br>$A.\overline{C}$ | 6<br>$\overline{A}$ | 7<br>$\overline{A}.B$ | 8<br>$\overline{A}.B.\overline{C}$ | 9<br>$Z = A.\overline{C} + \overline{A}.B + \overline{A}.B.\overline{C}$ |
|---|---|---|---|---|---|---|---|---|
| 0 | 0 | 0 | 1 | 0 | 1 | 0 | 0 | 0 |
| 0 | 0 | 1 | 0 | 0 | 1 | 0 | 0 | 0 |
| 0 | 1 | 0 | 1 | 0 | 1 | 1 | 1 | 1 |
| 0 | 1 | 1 | 0 | 0 | 1 | 1 | 0 | 1 |
| 1 | 0 | 0 | 1 | 1 | 0 | 0 | 0 | 1 |
| 1 | 0 | 1 | 0 | 0 | 0 | 0 | 0 | 0 |
| 1 | 1 | 0 | 1 | 1 | 0 | 0 | 0 | 1 |
| 1 | 1 | 1 | 0 | 0 | 0 | 0 | 0 | 0 |

The corresponding truth table is shown in *Fig 9(b)*.

Column 4 is $\bar{C}$, opposite to column 3.

Column 5 is $A.\bar{C}$, obtained by applying the **and**-function to columns 1 and 4.

Column 6 is $\bar{A}$, opposite to column 1.

Column 7 is $\bar{A}.B$, obtained by applying the **and**-function to columns 2 and 6.

Column 8 is $\bar{A}.B.\bar{C}$, obtained by applying the **and**-function to columns 4 and 7.

Column 9 is the output, obtained by applying the **or**-function to columns 5, 7 and 8.

*Problem 4*  Derive the Boolean equation and construct the switching circuit for the truth table given in *Fig 10(a)*.

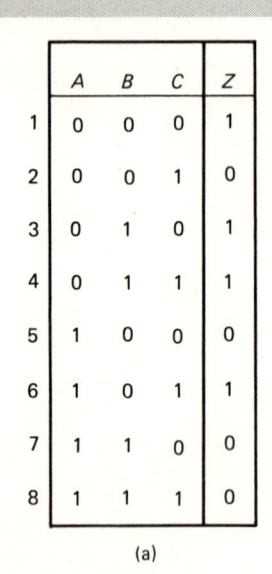

|   | A | B | C | Z |
|---|---|---|---|---|
| 1 | 0 | 0 | 0 | 1 |
| 2 | 0 | 0 | 1 | 0 |
| 3 | 0 | 1 | 0 | 1 |
| 4 | 0 | 1 | 1 | 1 |
| 5 | 1 | 0 | 0 | 0 |
| 6 | 1 | 0 | 1 | 1 |
| 7 | 1 | 1 | 0 | 0 |
| 8 | 1 | 1 | 1 | 0 |

(a)

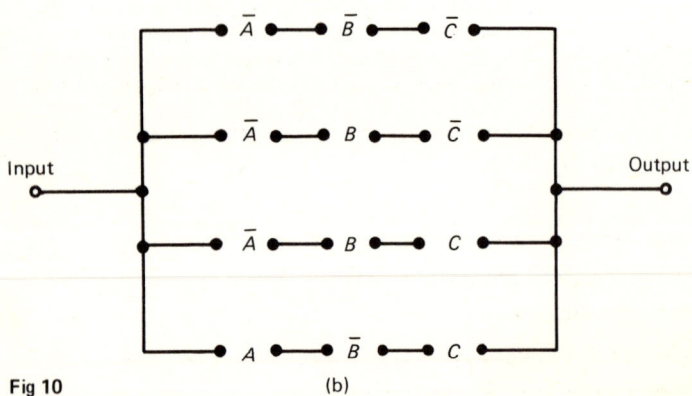

**Fig 10**                    (b)

Examination of the truth table shown in *Fig 10(a)* shows that there is a 1 output in the $Z$-column in rows 1, 3, 4 and 6. Thus, the Boolean expression and switching circuit should be such that a 1 output is obtained for row 1 or row 3 or row 4 or row 6. In row 1, $A$ is 0 and $B$ is 0 and $C$ is 0 and this corresponds to the Boolean expression $\overline{A}.\overline{B}.\overline{C}$. In row 3, $A$ is 0 and $B$ is 1 and $C$ is 0, i.e. the Boolean expression is $\overline{A}.B.\overline{C}$. Similarly in rows 4 and 6, the Boolean expressions are $\overline{A}.B.C$ and $A.\overline{B}.C$ respectively. Hence the Boolean equation is:

$$Z = \overline{A}.\overline{B}.\overline{C} + \overline{A}.B.\overline{C} + \overline{A}.B.C + A.\overline{B}.C$$

The corresponding switching circuit is shown in *Fig 8(b)*. The four terms are joined by **or**-functions $(+)$, and are represented by four parallel circuits. Each term has three elements joined by an **and**-function, and is represented by three elements connected in series.

*Problem 5* By constructing the appropriate truth table show that
$A + (B.C) = (A+B).(A+C)$

The truth table is shown in *Table 6*.

TABLE 6

| 1 | 2 | 3 | 4 | 5 | 6 | 7 | 8 |
|---|---|---|---|---|---|---|---|
| $A$ | $B$ | $C$ | $B.C$ | $(A+B.C)$ | $A+B$ | $A+C$ | $(A+B).(A+C)$ |
| 0 | 0 | 0 | 0 | 0 | 0 | 0 | 0 |
| 0 | 0 | 1 | 0 | 0 | 0 | 1 | 0 |
| 0 | 1 | 0 | 0 | 0 | 1 | 0 | 0 |
| 0 | 1 | 1 | 1 | 1 | 1 | 1 | 1 |
| 1 | 0 | 0 | 0 | 1 | 1 | 1 | 1 |
| 1 | 0 | 1 | 0 | 1 | 1 | 1 | 1 |
| 1 | 1 | 0 | 0 | 1 | 1 | 1 | 1 |
| 1 | 1 | 1 | 1 | 1 | 1 | 1 | 1 |

Columns 1, 2 and 3 are all the possible combinations of $A$, $B$ and $C$.
Column 4 is $B.C$, obtained by applying the **and**-function to columns 2 and 3.
Column 5 is $(A+B.C)$, obtained by applying the **or**-function to columns 1 and 4.
Column 6 is $(A+B)$, obtained by applying the **or**-function to columns 1 and 2.
Column 7 is $(A+C)$, obtained by applying the **or**-function to columns 1 and 3.
Column 8 is $(A+B).(A+C)$, obtained by applying the **and**-function to columns 6 and 7.
Since the pattern of 0's and 1's in columns 5 and 8 are the same, this shows that

$$A + (B.C) = (A+B).(A+C)$$

*Problem 6* Show that $A + \overline{A}.B = A + B$

In the truth table shown in *Table 7*, since columns 5 and 6 have the same pattern of 0's and 1's then

$$A + \overline{A}.B = A + B$$

TABLE 7

| 1<br>$A$ | 2<br>$B$ | 3<br>$\overline{A}$ | 4<br>$\overline{A}.B$ | 5<br>$A+\overline{A}.B$ | 6<br>$A+B$ |
|---|---|---|---|---|---|
| 0 | 0 | 1 | 0 | 0 | 0 |
| 0 | 1 | 1 | 1 | 1 | 1 |
| 1 | 0 | 0 | 0 | 1 | 1 |
| 1 | 1 | 0 | 0 | 1 | 1 |

*Problem 7* Simplify the Boolean expression: $\overline{P}.\overline{Q}+\overline{P}.Q+P.\overline{Q}$

The laws and rules of Boolean algebra given in *Table 2* are used to simplify Boolean expressions.

$$
\begin{aligned}
&\quad\quad\quad\quad\quad\quad\quad\quad\quad\quad\quad\quad\quad\quad\quad\quad\quad\quad\quad\quad\quad\quad\quad\textit{Reference}\\
\overline{P}.\overline{Q}+\overline{P}.Q+P.\overline{Q} &= \overline{P}.(\overline{Q}+Q)+P.\overline{Q} && 5\\
&= \overline{P}.1+P.\overline{Q} && 10\\
&= \boldsymbol{\overline{P}+P.\overline{Q}} && 12
\end{aligned}
$$

*Problem 8* Simplify $(P+\overline{P}.Q).(Q+\overline{Q}.P)$

With reference to *Table 2*:

$$
\begin{aligned}
&\quad\quad\quad\quad\quad\quad\quad\quad\quad\quad\quad\quad\quad\quad\quad\quad\quad\quad\quad\quad\quad\quad\quad\textit{Reference}\\
(P+\overline{P}.Q).(Q+\overline{Q}.P) &= P.(Q+\overline{Q}.P)+\overline{P}.Q.(Q+\overline{Q}.P) && 5\\
&= P.Q+P.\overline{Q}.P+\overline{P}.Q.Q+\overline{P}.Q.\overline{Q}.P && 5\\
&= P.Q+P.\overline{Q}+\overline{P}.Q+\overline{P}.Q.\overline{Q}.P && 13\\
&= P.Q+P.\overline{Q}+\overline{P}.Q+0 && 14\\
&= P.Q+P.\overline{Q}+\overline{P}.Q && 7\\
&= P.(Q+\overline{Q})+\overline{P}.Q && 5\\
&= P.1+\overline{P}.Q && 10\\
&= \boldsymbol{P+\overline{P}.Q} && 12
\end{aligned}
$$

*Problem 9* Simplify $F.G.\overline{H}+F.G.H+\overline{F}.G.H$

With reference to *Table 2*:

$$
\begin{aligned}
&\quad\quad\quad\quad\quad\quad\quad\quad\quad\quad\quad\quad\quad\quad\quad\quad\quad\quad\quad\quad\quad\textit{Reference}\\
F.G.\overline{H}+F.G.H+\overline{F}.G.H &= F.G.(\overline{H}+H)+\overline{F}.G.H && 5\\
&= F.G.1\quad\quad+\overline{F}.G.H && 10\\
&= F.G+\overline{F}.G.H && 12\\
&= \boldsymbol{G.(F+\overline{F}.H)} && 5
\end{aligned}
$$

*Problem 10* Simplify $\overline{F}.\overline{G}.H+\overline{F}.G.H+F.\overline{G}.H+F.G.H$

With reference to *Table 2*:

$$
\begin{aligned}
&\quad\quad\quad\quad\quad\quad\quad\quad\quad\quad\quad\quad\quad\quad\quad\quad\quad\quad\quad\quad\quad\quad\textit{Reference}\\
\overline{F}.\overline{G}.H+\overline{F}.G.H+F.\overline{G}.H+F.G.H &= \overline{G}.H.(\overline{F}+F)\quad+G.H.(\overline{F}+F) && 5\\
&= \overline{G}.H.1\quad\quad\quad+G.H.1 && 10\\
&= \overline{G}.H+G.H && 12\\
&= H.(\overline{G}+G) && 5\\
&= H.1\ =\ \boldsymbol{H} && \text{10 and 12}
\end{aligned}
$$

## C. FURTHER PROBLEMS ON BOOLEAN ALGEBRA AND SWITCHING CIRCUITS

In *Problems 1 to 4*, determine the Boolean expressions and construct truth tables for the switching circuits given.

1  The circuit shown in *Fig 11(a)*. $[C.(A.B+\overline{A}.B)$; see *Table* 8, col. 4]
2  The circuit shown in *Fig 11(b)*. $[C.(A.\overline{B}+\overline{A})$; see *Table* 8, col. 5]
3  The circuit shown in *Fig 11(c)*. $[A.B.(B.\overline{C}+\overline{B}.C+\overline{A}.B)$; see *Table* 8, col. 6]
4  The circuit shown in *Fig 11(d)*. $[C.[B.C.\overline{A}+A.(B+\overline{C})]$, see *Table* 8, col. 7]

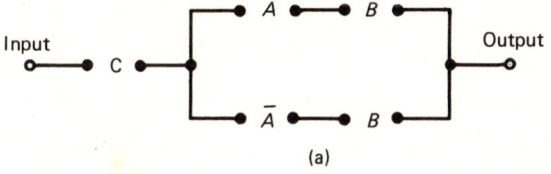

(a)

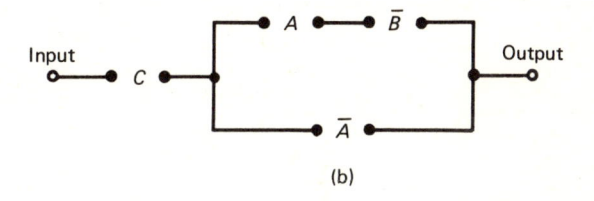

(b)

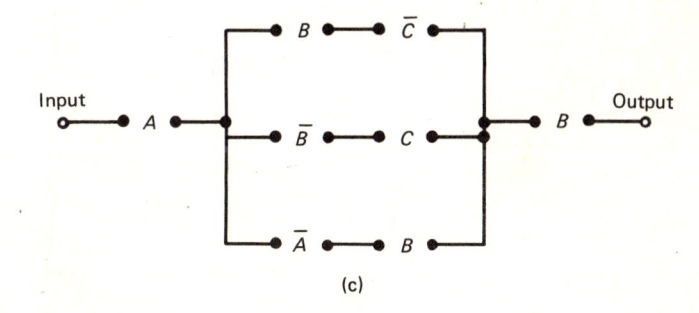

(c)

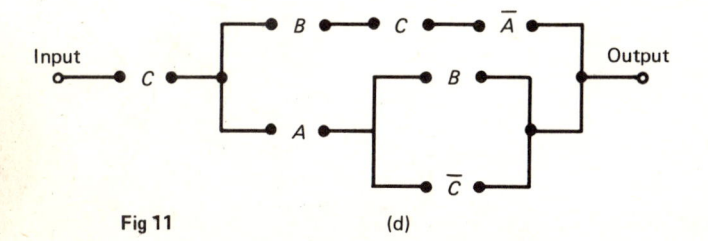

**Fig 11** (d)

TABLE 8

| 1<br>$A$ | 2<br>$B$ | 3<br>$C$ | 4<br>$C.(A.B+\overline{A}.B)$ | 5<br>$C.(A.\overline{B}+\overline{A})$ | 6<br>$A.B(B.\overline{C}+\overline{B}.C+\overline{A}.B)$ | 7<br>$C.[B.C.\overline{A}+A.\ (B+\overline{C})]$ |
|---|---|---|---|---|---|---|
| 0 | 0 | 0 | 0 | 0 | 0 | 0 |
| 0 | 0 | 1 | 0 | 1 | 0 | 0 |
| 0 | 1 | 0 | 0 | 0 | 0 | 0 |
| 0 | 1 | 1 | 1 | 1 | 0 | 1 |
| 1 | 0 | 0 | 0 | 0 | 0 | 0 |
| 1 | 0 | 1 | 0 | 1 | 0 | 0 |
| 1 | 1 | 0 | 0 | 0 | 1 | 0 |
| 1 | 1 | 1 | 1 | 0 | 0 | 1 |

In *Problems 5 to 7*, construct switching circuits to meet the requirements of the Boolean expressions given.

5  $A.C+A.\overline{B}.C+A.B$               [See *Fig 12(a)*]

6  $A.B.C.(A+B+C)$                [See *Fig 12(b)*]

7  $A.\ (A.\overline{B}.C+B.(A+\overline{C}))$      [See *Fig 12(c)*]

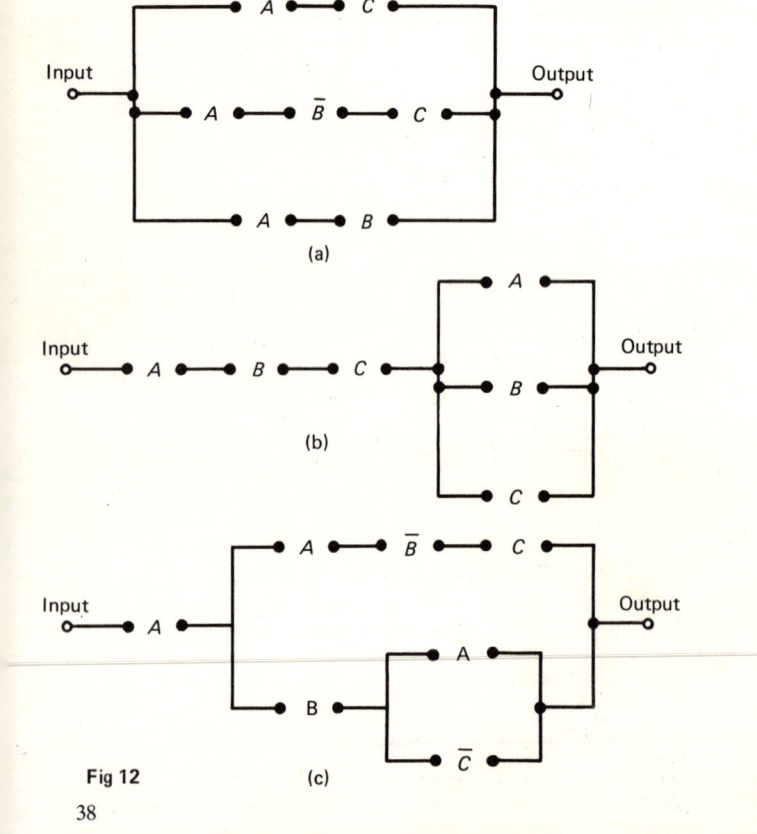

Fig 12

38

TABLE 9

| 1 | 2 | 3 | 4 | 5 | 6 |
|---|---|---|---|---|---|
| A | B | C |   |   |   |
| 0 | 0 | 0 | 0 | 1 | 1 |
| 0 | 0 | 1 | 1 | 0 | 0 |
| 0 | 1 | 0 | 0 | 0 | 1 |
| 0 | 1 | 1 | 0 | 1 | 0 |
| 1 | 0 | 0 | 0 | 1 | 1 |
| 1 | 0 | 1 | 0 | 0 | 1 |
| 1 | 1 | 0 | 1 | 0 | 0 |
| 1 | 1 | 1 | 0 | 0 | 0 |

In *Problems 8 to 10*, derive the Boolean expressions and construct the switching circuits for the truth table stated.

8  *Table 9*, column 4.                    $[\overline{A}.\overline{B}.C+A.B.\overline{C}$; see *Fig 13(a)*]
9  *Table 9*, column 5.                    $[\overline{A}.\overline{B}.\overline{C}+\overline{A}.B.C+A.\overline{B}.\overline{C}$; see *Fig 13(b)*]
10  *Table 9*, column 6.                    $[\overline{A}.\overline{B}.\overline{C}+\overline{A}.B.\overline{C}+A.\overline{B}.\overline{C}+A.\overline{B}.C$; see *Fig 13(c)*]

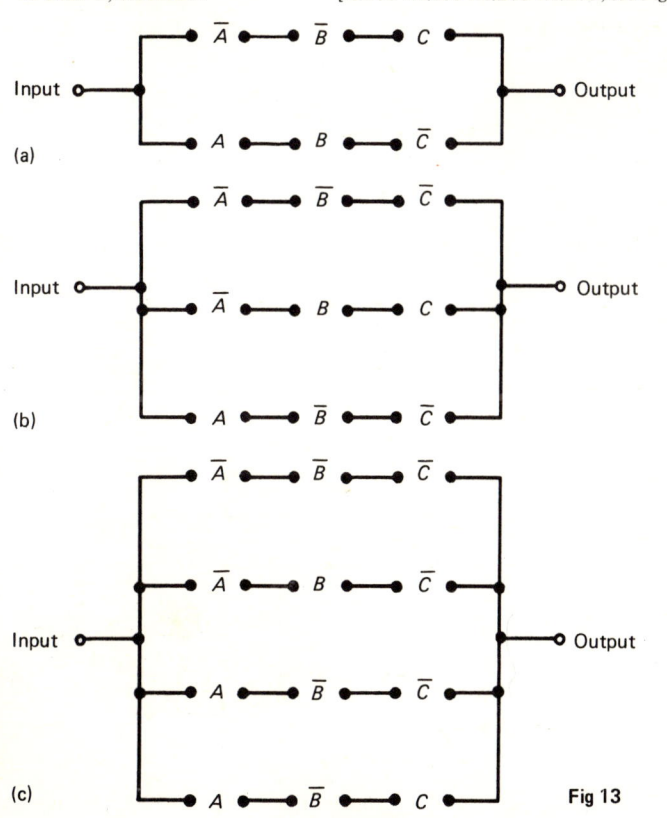

Fig 13

In *Problems 11 to 13*, show that the relationships given are true by means of a truth table.

11 $(\overline{A}+B) . (\overline{A}+C) = \overline{A}+B.C$

12 $\overline{A}+A.\overline{B} = \overline{A}+\overline{B}$

13 $A+A.B = A$

In *Problems 14 to 25*, use the laws and rules of Boolean algebra to simplify the expressions given.

| | | |
|---|---|---|
| 14 $\overline{P}.\overline{Q}+\overline{P}.Q$ | | $[\overline{P}]$ |
| 15 $\overline{P}.Q+P.Q$ | | $[Q]$ |
| 16 $\overline{P}.Q+P.Q+\overline{P}.\overline{Q}$ | | $[\overline{P}+P.Q]$ |
| 17 $P.\overline{P}.Q+P.Q.\overline{Q}$ | | $[0]$ |
| 18 $(P+P.Q) . (Q+Q.P)$ | | $[P.Q]$ |
| 19 $\overline{F}.\overline{G}.\overline{H}+\overline{F}.\overline{G}.H$ | | $[\overline{F}.\overline{G}]$ |
| 20 $\overline{F}.G.H+F.G.H$ | | $[G.H]$ |
| 21 $\overline{F}.\overline{G}.H+\overline{F}.G.H+F.\overline{G}.H$ | | $[H.(\overline{F}+F.\overline{G})]$ |
| 22 $F.\overline{G}.\overline{H}+F.G.H+\overline{F}.G.H$ | | $[F.\overline{G}.\overline{H}+G.H]$ |
| 23 $\overline{F}.\overline{G}.\overline{H}+\overline{F}.\overline{G}.H+F.\overline{G}.\overline{H}+F.\overline{G}.H$ | | $[\overline{G}]$ |
| 24 $\overline{F}.G.H+\overline{F}.G.H+F.G.H+F.\overline{G}.H$ | | $[H.(\overline{F}.G+F)]$ |
| 25 $F.\overline{G}.H+F.G.H+F.G.\overline{H}+\overline{F}.G.\overline{H}$ | | $[F.H+G.\overline{H}]$ |

# 5 Logic circuits

## A. MAIN POINTS CONCERNED WITH LOGIC CIRCUITS

1  In practice, logic gates are used to perform the **and, or** and **not** functions introduced in Chapter 4. Logic gates can be made from switches, magnetic devices of fluidic devices, but most logic gates in use are electronic devices. Various logic gates are available. For example, the Boolean expression $(A.B.C)$ can be produced using a three-input, **and**-gate and $(C+D)$ by using a two-input **or**-gate. The principal gates in common use are introduced in paras 2 to 6. The term 'gate' is used in the same sense as a normal gate, the open state being indicated by a binary '1' and the closed state by a binary '0'. A gate will only open when the requirements of the gate are met and, for example, there will only be a '1' output on a two-input **and**-gate when both the inputs to the gate are at a '1' state.

2  The **and**-gate.
Two different symbols used for a three-input, **and**-gate are shown in *Fig 1(a)* and

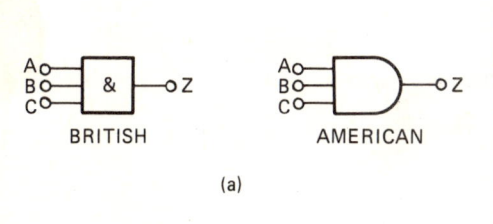

BRITISH  AMERICAN

(a)

| INPUTS | | | OUTPUT |
| A | B | C | Z = A.B.C |
|---|---|---|---|
| 0 | 0 | 0 | 0 |
| 0 | 0 | 1 | 0 |
| 0 | 1 | 0 | 0 |
| 0 | 1 | 1 | 0 |
| 1 | 0 | 0 | 0 |
| 1 | 0 | 1 | 0 |
| 1 | 1 | 0 | 0 |
| 1 | 1 | 1 | 1 |

**Fig 1**  (b)

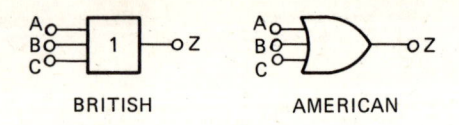

BRITISH AMERICAN

(a)

| INPUTS | | | OUTPUT |
|---|---|---|---|
| A | B | C | Z = A+B+C |
| 0 | 0 | 0 | 0 |
| 0 | 0 | 1 | 1 |
| 0 | 1 | 0 | 1 |
| 0 | 1 | 1 | 1 |
| 1 | 0 | 0 | 1 |
| 1 | 0 | 1 | 1 |
| 1 | 1 | 0 | 1 |
| 1 | 1 | 1 | 1 |

**Fig 2** (b)

the truth table is shown in *Fig 1(b)*. This shows that there will only be a '1' output when $A$ is 1 and $B$ is 1 and $C$ is 1, written as:

$$Z = A.B.C.$$

3. The **or**-gate.
   Two different symbols used for a three-input **or**-gate are shown in *Fig 2(a)* and the truth table is shown in *Fig 2(b)*. This shows that there will be a '1' output when $A$ is 1, or $B$ is 1, or $C$ is 1, or any combinations of $A$, $B$ or $C$ is 1, written as $Z = A+B+C$.

4. The **invert**-gate or **not**-gate.
   Two different symbols used for an **invert**-gate are shown in *Fig 3(a)* and the truth table is shown in *Fig 3(b)*. This shows that a '0' input gives a '1' output and vice versa, i.e. it is an 'opposite to' function. The invert of $A$ is written $\overline{A}$ and is called 'not-$A$'.

5. The **nand**-gate.
   Two different symbols used for a **nand**-gate are shown in *Fig 4(a)* and the truth table is shown in *Fig 4(b)*. This gate is equivalent to an **and**-gate and an **invert**-gate in series (not-and = nand) and the output is written as $Z = \overline{A.B.C}$.

6. The **nor**-gate.
   Two different symbols used for a **nor**-gate are shown in *Fig 5(a)* and the truth

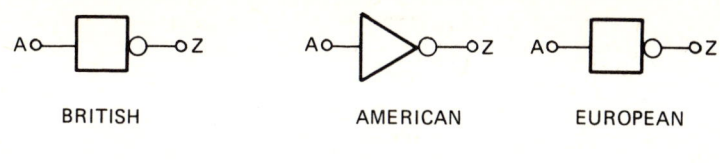

BRITISH AMERICAN EUROPEAN

(a)

| INPUT A | OUTPUT $Z=\overline{A}$ |
|---------|------------------------|
| 0 | 1 |
| 1 | 0 |

Fig 3

(b)

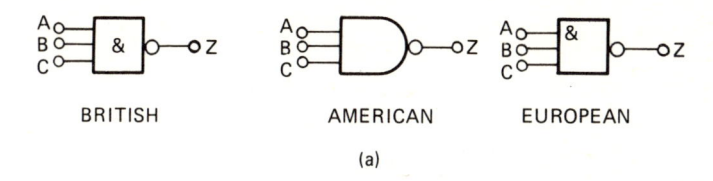

BRITISH AMERICAN EUROPEAN

(a)

| INPUTS | | | A.B.C. | OUTPUT $Z=\overline{A.B.C.}$ |
|---|---|---|---|---|
| A | B | C | | |
| 0 | 0 | 0 | 0 | 1 |
| 0 | 0 | 1 | 0 | 1 |
| 0 | 1 | 0 | 0 | 1 |
| 0 | 1 | 1 | 0 | 1 |
| 1 | 0 | 0 | 0 | 1 |
| 1 | 0 | 1 | 0 | 1 |
| 1 | 1 | 0 | 0 | 1 |
| 1 | 1 | 1 | 1 | 0 |

Fig 4

(b)

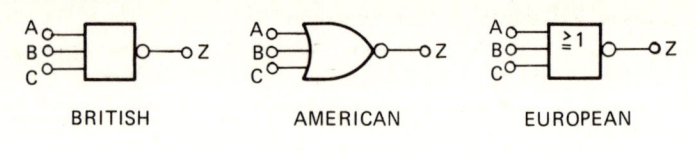

BRITISH  AMERICAN  EUROPEAN

(a)

| INPUTS | | | A+B+C | OUTPUT |
| A | B | C | | $Z = \overline{A+B+C}$ |
|---|---|---|---|---|
| 0 | 0 | 0 | 0 | 1 |
| 0 | 0 | 1 | 1 | 0 |
| 0 | 1 | 0 | 1 | 0 |
| 0 | 1 | 1 | 1 | 0 |
| 1 | 0 | 0 | 1 | 0 |
| 1 | 0 | 1 | 1 | 0 |
| 1 | 1 | 0 | 1 | 0 |
| 1 | 1 | 1 | 1 | 0 |

**Fig 5**

(b)

table is shown in *Fig 5(b)*. This gate is equivalent to an **or**-gate and an **invert**-gate in series, (not-or = nor), and the output is written as: $Z = \overline{A+B+C}$.

7 Combinational logic networks.

In most logic circuits, more than one gate is needed to give the required output. Except for the **invert**-gate, logic gates generally have two, three or four inputs and are confined to one function only, thus, for example, a two-input, **or**-gate or a four-input **and**-gate can be used when designing a logic circuit. The way in which logic gates are used to generate a given output is shown in *Problems 1 to 4*.

8 Universal logic gates.

The function of any of the five logic gates in common use can be obtained by using either **nand**-gates or **nor**-gates and when used in this manner, the gate selected is called a **universal gate**. The way in which universal **nand**-gates are used to produce the **invert, and, or** and **nor**-functions is shown in *Problems 5 and 7*. The way in which universal **nor**-gates are used to produce the **invert, or, and** and **nand**-functions is shown in *Problems 6 and 8*. A practical problem on the use of logic gates is given in *Problem 9*.

## B. WORKED PROBLEMS ON LOGIC CIRCUITS

*Problem 1*  Devise a logic system to meet the requirements of:

$$Z = A.\bar{B} + C$$

With reference to *Fig 6* an **invert**-gate, shown as (1), gives $\bar{B}$. The **and**-gate shown as (2), has input of $A$ and $\bar{B}$, giving $A.\bar{B}$. The **or**-gate, shown as (3), has inputs of $A.\bar{B}$ and $C$, giving $Z = A.\bar{B} + C$.

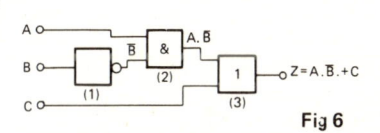

Fig 6

*Problem 2*  Devise a logic system to meet the requirements of:

$$(P+\bar{Q}) . (\bar{R}+S)$$

The logic system is shown in *Fig 7*. The given expression shows that two **invert**-functions are needed to give $\bar{Q}$ and $\bar{R}$ and these are shown as gates (1) and (2). Two **or**-gates, shown as (3) and (4), give $(P+\bar{Q})$ and $(\bar{R}+S)$ respectively. Finally, an **and**-gate, shown as (5), gives the required output, $Z = (P+\bar{Q}) . (\bar{R}+S)$.

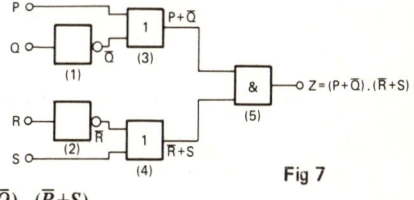

Fig 7

*Problem 3*  Devise a logic circuit to meet the requirements of the output given in *Table 1*, using as few gates as possible.

TABLE 1

| | Inputs | | Output |
|---|---|---|---|
| A | B | C | Z |
| 0 | 0 | 0 | 0 |
| 0 | 0 | 1 | 0 |
| 0 | 1 | 0 | 0 |
| 0 | 1 | 1 | 0 |
| 1 | 0 | 0 | 0 |
| 1 | 0 | 1 | 1 |
| 1 | 1 | 0 | 1 |
| 1 | 1 | 1 | 1 |

The '1' outputs in rows 6, 7 and 8 of *Table 1* show that the Boolean expression is: $Z = A.\bar{B}.C + A.B.\bar{C} + A.B.C$. The logic circuit for this expression can be built using three 3-input **and**-gates and one 3-input **or**-gate, together with two **invert**-gates. However, the number of gates required can be reduced by using the techniques introduced in Chapter 4, resulting in the cost of the circuit being reduced.

Using the laws and rules of Boolean algebra,
(see Chapter 4, *Table 2*), page 29

$$Z = A.\overline{B}.C + A.B.\overline{C} + A.B.C$$
$$= A.[\overline{B}.C + B.\overline{C} + B.C]$$
$$= A.[\overline{B}.C + B.(\overline{C} + C)]$$
$$= A.[\overline{B}.C + B]$$
$$= A.[B + \overline{B}.C]. \text{ But from Chapter 4, } Problem \ 6, \text{ page 36 } A + \overline{A}.B = A + B$$

Hence $Z = A.(B + C)$.

The logic circuit to give this simplified expression is shown in *Fig 8*.

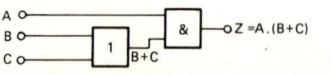

**Fig 8**

*Problem 4* Simplify the expression:

$$Z = \overline{P}.\overline{Q}.\overline{R}.\overline{S} + \overline{P}.\overline{Q}.\overline{R}.S + \overline{P}.Q.\overline{R}.\overline{S} + \overline{P}.Q.\overline{R}.S + P.\overline{Q}.\overline{R}.\overline{S}$$

and devise a logic circuit to give this output.

Applying the rules of Boolean algebra given in Chapter 4, *Table 2*, page 29

$$Z = \overline{P}.\overline{Q}.\overline{R}.(\overline{S} + S) + \overline{P}.Q.\overline{R}.(\overline{S} + S) + P.\overline{Q}.\overline{R}.\overline{S}$$

and since $\overline{S} + S = 1$ and $A.1 = A$, then

$$Z = \overline{P}.\overline{Q}.\overline{R} + \overline{P}.Q.\overline{R} + P.\overline{Q}.\overline{R}.\overline{S}$$
$$= \overline{Q}.\overline{R}.(\overline{P} + P.\overline{S}) + \overline{P}.Q.\overline{R}$$

But from *Problem 6*, Chapter 4, page 36 $A + \overline{A}.B = A + B$, hence

$$(\overline{P} + P.\overline{S}) = (\overline{P} + \overline{S}), \text{ hence}$$
$$Z = \overline{Q}.\overline{R}.(\overline{P} + \overline{S}) + \overline{P}.Q.\overline{R}$$
$$= \overline{P}.\overline{Q}.\overline{R} + \overline{Q}.\overline{R}.\overline{S} + \overline{P}.Q.\overline{R}$$
$$= \overline{R}.(\overline{P}.\overline{Q} + \overline{Q}.\overline{S} + \overline{P}.Q)$$
$$= \overline{R}.[\overline{P}.(\overline{Q} + Q) + \overline{Q}.\overline{S}]$$
$$= \overline{R}.(\overline{P} + \overline{Q}.\overline{S})$$

Thus the simplified expression is $Z = \overline{R}.(\overline{P} + \overline{Q}.\overline{S})$.

The logic circuit to produce this expression is shown in *Fig 9*.

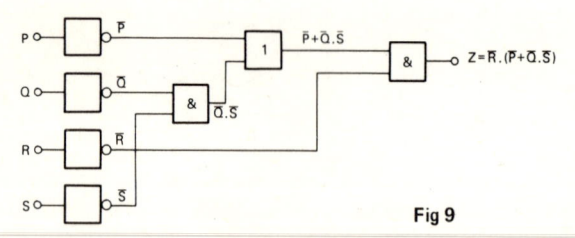

**Fig 9**

*Problem 5* Show how **invert, and, or** and **nor**-functions can be produced using **nand**-gates only.

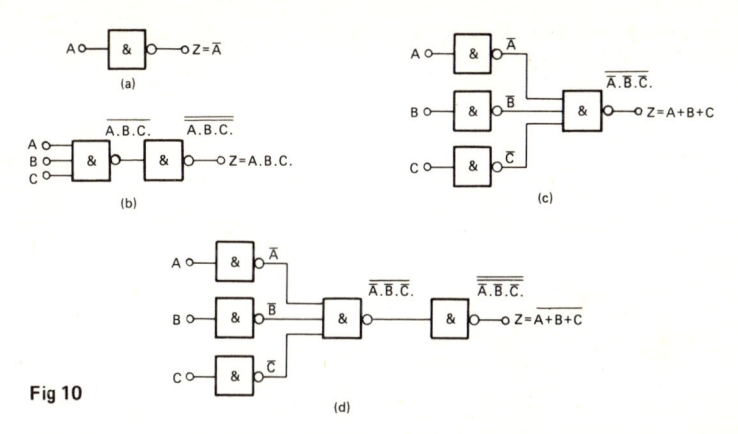

**Fig 10**

A single input to a **nand**-gate gives the **invert**-function, as shown in *Fig 10(a)*. When two **nand**-gates are connected, as shown in *Fig 10(b)*, the output from the first gate is $\overline{A.B.C}$ and this is inverted by the second gate, giving $Z = \overline{\overline{A.B.C}} = A.B.C$, i.e. the **and-function** is produced. When $\overline{A}$, $\overline{B}$ and $\overline{C}$ are the inputs to a **nand**-gate, the output is $\overline{\overline{A}.\overline{B}.\overline{C}}$. Two important laws for dealing with expressions such as these are **de Morgan's laws**, which state that $\overline{A.B} = \overline{A} + \overline{B}$ and $\overline{A+B} = \overline{A}.\overline{B}$. (Proved easily using a truth table.)  By de Morgan's law, $\overline{A.B.C} = \overline{A} + \overline{B} + \overline{C} = A+B+C$, i.e. a **nand**-gate is used to produce the **or**-function. The logic circuit is shown in *Fig 10(c)*. If the output from the logic circuit in *Fig 10(c)* is inverted by adding an additional **nand**-gate, the output becomes the invert of an **or**-function, i.e. the **nor**-function, as shown in *Fig 10(d)*.

*Problem 6* Show how **invert, or, and** and **nand**-functions can be produced by using **nor**-gates only.

A single input to a **nor**-gate gives the **invert**-function, as shown in *Fig 11(a)*. When two **nor**-gates are connected, as shown in *Fig 11(b)*, the output from the first gate is $\overline{A+B+C}$ and this is inverted by the second gate, giving $Z = \overline{\overline{A+B+C}} = A+B+C$,

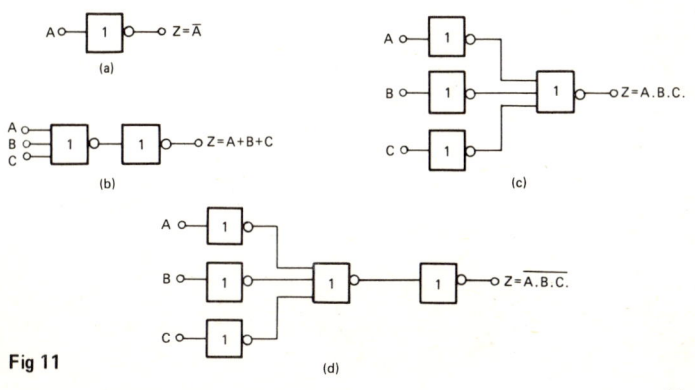

**Fig 11**

i.e. the or-function is produced. Inputs of $\overline{A}$, $\overline{B}$ and $\overline{C}$ to a nor-gate give an output of $\overline{\overline{A}+\overline{B}+\overline{C}}$. By de Morgan's law: $\overline{\overline{A}+\overline{B}+\overline{C}} = \overline{\overline{A}}.\overline{\overline{B}}.\overline{\overline{C}} = A.B.C$, i.e., the nor-gate can be used to produce the and-function. The logic circuit is shown in *Fig 11(c)*. When the output of the logic circuit, shown in *Fig 11(c)*, is inverted by adding an additional nor-gate, the output then becomes the invert of an or-function, i.e. the nor-function as shown in *Fig 11(d)*.

---

*Problem 7* Design a logic circuit, using nand-gates having not more than three inputs, to meet the requirements of the Boolean equation:

$$Z = \overline{A} + \overline{B} + C + \overline{D}.$$

---

When designing logic circuits, it is often easier to start at the output of the circuit. The given expression shows there are four variables, joined by or-functions. From the principles introduced in *Problem 5*, if a four-input nand-gate is used to give the required expression, the inputs are $\overline{\overline{A}}$, $\overline{B}$, $\overline{C}$ and $\overline{\overline{D}}$, that is, $A$, $B$, $\overline{C}$ and $D$. However, the problem states that three-inputs are not to be exceeded, so two of the variables

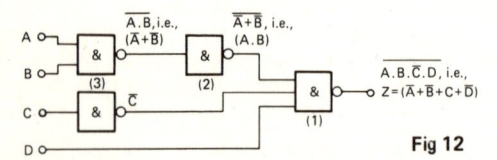

**Fig 12**

are joined, the inputs to the three-input nand-gate, shown as gate (1) in *Fig 12*, is $A.B$, $\overline{C}$ and $D$. From *Problem 5*, the and-function is generated by using two nand-gates connected in series, shown by gates (2) and (3) in *Fig 12*. The logic circuit required to produce the given equation is as shown in *Fig 12*.

---

*Problem 8* Use nor-gates only to design a logic circuit to meet the requirements of the equation: $Z = \overline{D}.(\overline{A}+B+\overline{C})$.

---

It is usual in logic circuit design to start the design at the output. From *Problem 6*, the and-function between $\overline{D}$ and the terms in the bracket can be produced by using inputs of $\overline{D}$ and $\overline{A}+B+\overline{C}$ to a nor-gate, i.e. by de Morgan's law, inputs of $D$ and

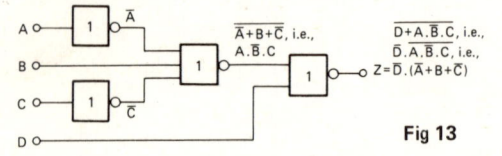

**Fig 13**

$A.\overline{B}.C$. Again, with reference to *Problem 6*, inputs of $\overline{A}.B$ and $\overline{C}$ to a nor-gate give an output of $\overline{A}+B+\overline{C}$, which by de Morgan's law is $A.\overline{B}.C$. The logic circuit to produce the required equation is as shown in *Fig 13*.

---

*Problem 9* An alarm indicator in a grinding mill complex should be activated if (a) the power supply to all mills is off and (b) the hopper feeding the mills is less than 10% full, and (c) if less than two of the three grinding mills are in action. Devise a logic system to meet these requirements.

Let variable $A$ represent the power supply on to all the mills, then $\overline{A}$ represents the power supply off. Let $B$ represent the hopper feeding the mills being more than 10% full, then $\overline{B}$ represents the hopper being less than 10% full. Let $C$, $D$ and $E$ represent the three mills respectively being in action, then $\overline{C}$, $\overline{D}$ and $\overline{E}$ represent the three mills respectively not being in action. The required equation to activate the alarm is:

$$Z = \overline{A}.\overline{B}.(\overline{C}+\overline{D}+\overline{E}).$$

There are three variables joined by **and**-functions in the output, indicating that a three-input **and**-gate is required, having inputs of $\overline{A}$, $\overline{B}$ and $(\overline{C}+\overline{D}+\overline{E})$. The term

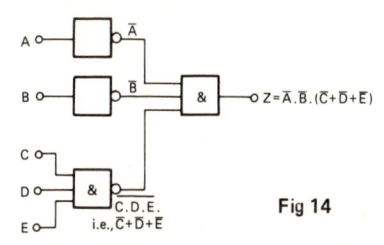

**Fig 14**

$(\overline{C}+\overline{D}+\overline{E})$ is produced by a three-input **nand**-gate. When variables $C$, $D$ and $E$ are the inputs to a **nand**-gate, the output is $\overline{C.D.E}$, which, by de Morgan's law is $\overline{C}+\overline{D}+\overline{E}$. Hence the required logic circuit is as shown in *Fig 14*.

## C. WORKED PROBLEMS ON LOGIC CIRCUITS

In *Problems 1 to 5*, devise logic systems to meet the requirements of the Boolean equations given.

1   $Z = \overline{A}+B.C$                                           [See *Fig 15(a)*]
2   $Z = A.\overline{B}+B.\overline{C}$                                      [See *Fig 15(b)*]
3   $Z = A.B.\overline{C}+\overline{A}.\overline{B}.C$                               [See *Fig 15(c)*]
4   $Z = (\overline{A}+B).(\overline{C}+D)$                                   [See *Fig 15(d)*]
5   $Z = A.\overline{B}+B.\overline{C}+C.\overline{D}$                            [See *Fig 15(e)*]

In *Problems 6 to 8*, simplify the expression given in the truth table and devise a logic circuit to meet the requirements stated.

6   Column 4, *Table 2*.                                      [$A.B+C$, see *Fig 16(a)*]

TABLE 2

| 1 | 2 | 3 | 4 | 5 | 6 |
|---|---|---|---|---|---|
| A | B | C | $Z_1$ | $Z_2$ | $Z_3$ |
| 0 | 0 | 0 | 0 | 0 | 0 |
| 0 | 0 | 1 | 1 | 0 | 0 |
| 0 | 1 | 0 | 0 | 0 | 1 |
| 0 | 1 | 1 | 1 | 1 | 1 |
| 1 | 0 | 0 | 0 | 1 | 0 |
| 1 | 0 | 1 | 1 | 1 | 1 |
| 1 | 1 | 0 | 1 | 0 | 1 |
| 1 | 1 | 1 | 1 | 1 | 1 |

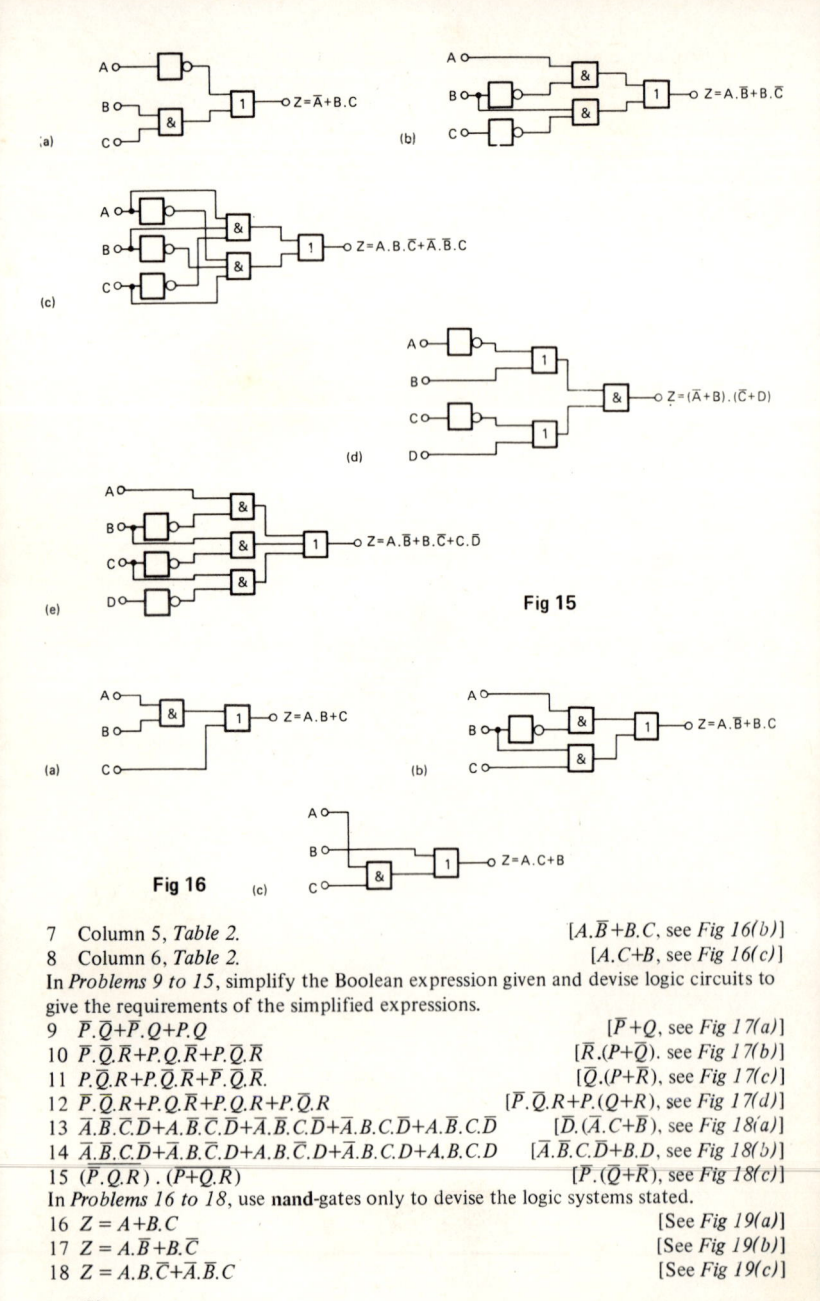

Fig 15

Fig 16

7  Column 5, *Table 2*.  $[A.\overline{B}+B.C$, see *Fig 16(b)*]
8  Column 6, *Table 2*.  $[A.C+B$, see *Fig 16(c)*]

In *Problems 9 to 15*, simplify the Boolean expression given and devise logic circuits to give the requirements of the simplified expressions.

9  $\overline{P}.\overline{Q}+\overline{P}.Q+P.Q$  $[\overline{P}+Q$, see *Fig 17(a)*]
10  $\overline{P}.\overline{Q}.\overline{R}+P.Q.\overline{R}+P.\overline{Q}.\overline{R}$  $[\overline{R}.(P+\overline{Q})$. see *Fig 17(b)*]
11  $P.\overline{Q}.R+P.\overline{Q}.\overline{R}+\overline{P}.\overline{Q}.R$.  $[\overline{Q}.(P+\overline{R})$, see *Fig 17(c)*]
12  $\overline{P}.\overline{Q}.R+P.Q.\overline{R}+P.Q.R+P.\overline{Q}.R$  $[\overline{P}.\overline{Q}.R+P.(Q+R)$, see *Fig 17(d)*]
13  $\overline{A}.\overline{B}.\overline{C}.\overline{D}+A.\overline{B}.\overline{C}.\overline{D}+\overline{A}.\overline{B}.C.\overline{D}+\overline{A}.B.C.\overline{D}+A.B.C.\overline{D}$  $[\overline{D}.(\overline{A}.C+\overline{B})$, see *Fig 18(a)*]
14  $\overline{A}.\overline{B}.C.\overline{D}+\overline{A}.B.\overline{C}.D+A.B.\overline{C}.D+\overline{A}.B.C.D+A.B.C.D$  $[\overline{A}.\overline{B}.C.\overline{D}+B.D$, see *Fig 18(b)*]
15  $(\overline{P}.Q.R).(\overline{P}+Q.\overline{R})$  $[\overline{P}.(\overline{Q}+\overline{R})$, see *Fig 18(c)*]

In *Problems 16 to 18*, use **nand**-gates only to devise the logic systems stated.

16  $Z = A+B.C$  [See *Fig 19(a)*]
17  $Z = A.\overline{B}+B.\overline{C}$  [See *Fig 19(b)*]
18  $Z = A.B.\overline{C}+\overline{A}.\overline{B}.C$  [See *Fig 19(c)*]

50

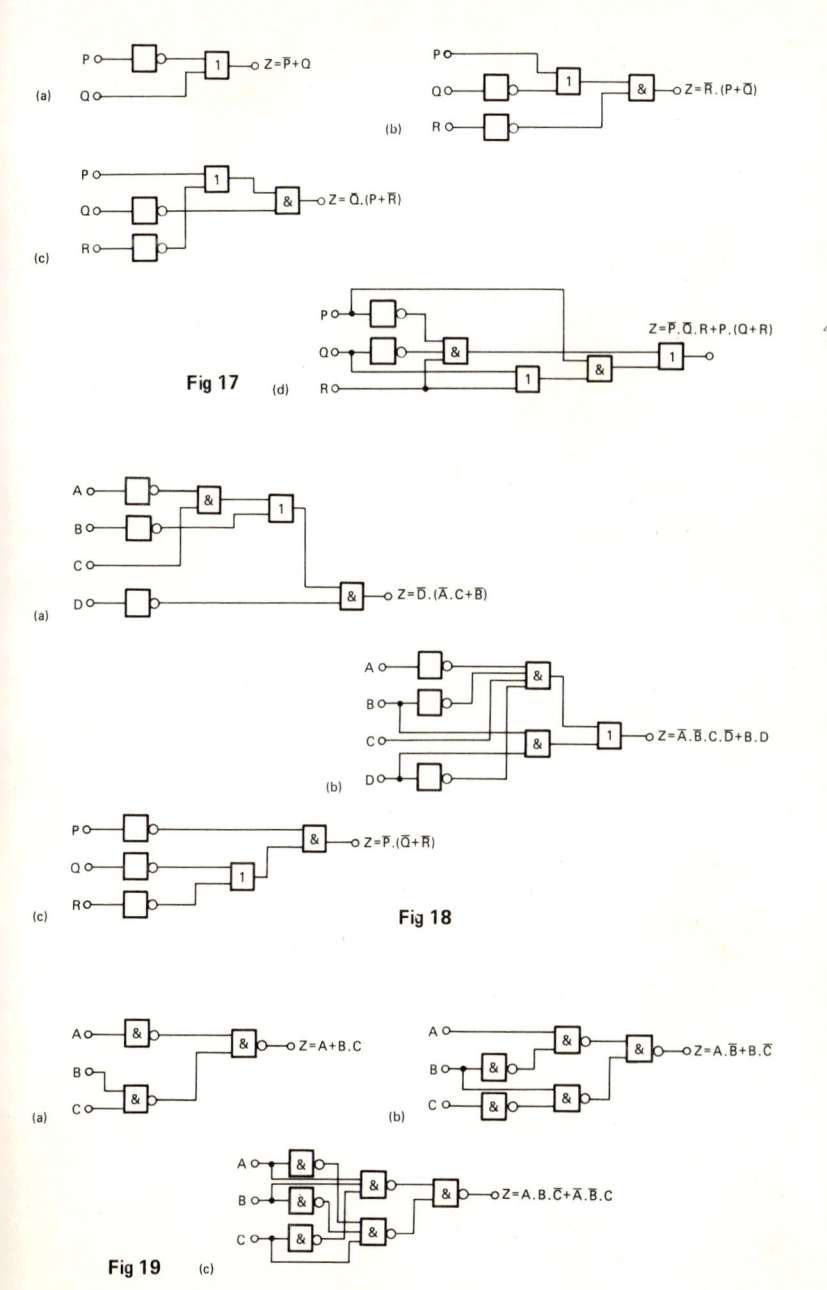

**Fig 17**

(a) $Z = \bar{P} + Q$

(b) $Z = \bar{R}.(P + \bar{Q})$

(c) $Z = \bar{Q}.(P + \bar{R})$

(d) $Z = \bar{P}.\bar{Q}.R + P.(Q + R)$

**Fig 18**

(a) $Z = \bar{D}.(\bar{A}.C + \bar{B})$

(b) $Z = \bar{A}.\bar{B}.C.\bar{D} + B.D$

(c) $Z = \bar{P}.(\bar{Q} + \bar{R})$

**Fig 19**

(a) $Z = A + B.C$

(b) $Z = A.\bar{B} + B.\bar{C}$

(c) $Z = A.B.\bar{C} + \bar{A}.\bar{B}.C$

51

In *Problems 19 to 21*, use **nor**-gates only to devise the logic systems stated.

19 $Z = (\overline{A}+B) \cdot (\overline{C}+D)$       [See *Fig 20(a)*]

20 $Z = A.\overline{B}+B.\overline{C}+C.\overline{D}$       [See *Fig 20(b)*]

21 $Z = \overline{P}.Q+P.(Q+R)$       [See *Fig 20(c)*]

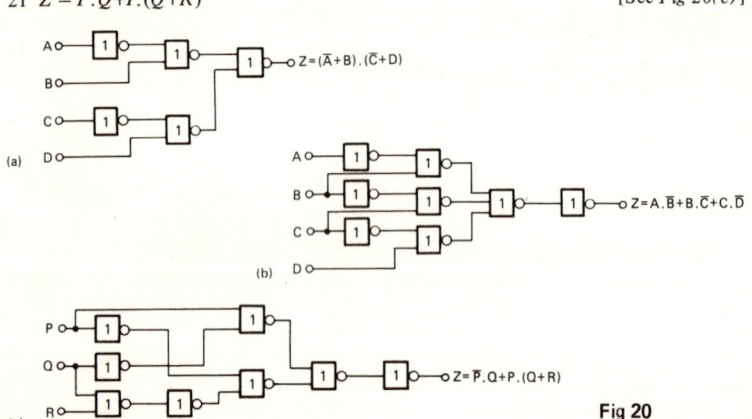

**Fig 20**

22 In a chemical process, three of the transducers used are *P, Q* and *R*, giving output signals of either 0 or 1. Devise a logic system to give a 1 output when:

(a) *P* and *Q* and *R* all have 0 outputs, or when:

(b) *P* is 0 and (*Q* is 1 or *R* is 0).       $[\overline{P}.(Q+R)$, see *Fig 21(a)*]

23 Lift doors should close, if:

(a) the master switch, (*A*), is on and either

(b) a call, (*B*), is received from any other floor, or

(c) the doors, (*C*), have been open for more than 10 seconds, or

(d) the selector push within the lift (*D*), is pressed for another floor.

Devise a logic circuit to meet these requirements.

$[Z = A.(B+C+D)$, see *Fig 21(b)*]

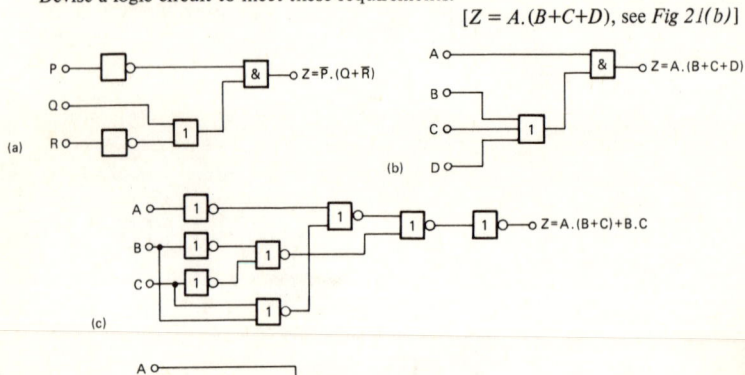

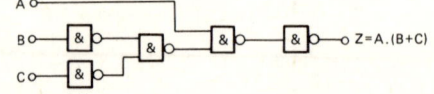

**Fig 21**

24 A water tank feeds three separate processes. When any two of the processes are in operation at the same time, a signal is required to start a pump to maintain the head of water in the tank. Devise a logic circuit using **nor**-gates only to give the required signal. $[Z = A.(B+C)+B.C$, see *Fig 21(c)*]

25 A logic signal is required to give an indication when:
   (a) the supply to an oven is on, and
   (b) the temperature of the oven exceeds $210°C$, or
   (c) the temperature of the oven is less than $190°C$.
   Devise a logic circuit using **nand**-gates only to meet these requirements.
   $[Z = A.(B+C)$, see *Fig 21(d)*]

# Index

101 101 − 110 110

$$\begin{array}{r} 001\ 001 \\ 1 \\ \hline 001\ 010 \end{array}$$

$$\begin{array}{r} 101\ 101 \\ 001\ 010 \\ \hline 110\ 111 \\ 001\ 00 \end{array}$$